Rostock, City by the Sea

The Story of a Young German

Peter Haase

Outskirts Press, Inc.
Denver, Colorado

Rostock, City by the Sea
The Story of a Young German
All Rights Reserved
Copyright © 2006 Peter Haase

Outskirts Press
http://www.outskirtspress.com

ISBN-10: 1-59800-662-2
ISBN-13: 978-1-59800-662-9

Cover photo by Linda Gruner
Cover design by Carlos Haase

Outskirts Press and the "OP" logo are trademarks belonging to
Outskirts Press, Inc.

Printed in the United States of America

Table of Contents

Acknowledgements

I am grateful for the assistance I have received from the accomplished writers of the Morningside and Fort Pierce, Florida, Groups who have constantly encouraged and motivated me to continue writing.

I owe my thanks to Almut and Bert Metzroth for meticulously editing my manuscript for historical correctness and stylistic improvement.

Last, but certainly not least, I thank Hans-Werner Bohl of the Rostocker Stadtarchiv for allowing me to translate and use excerpts from his book BOMBEN AUF ROSTOCK.

In Memory Of

My parents
Richard and Gertrud Haase
And my brother Dieter

PART ONE
Remembering Rostock

The Grüner Weg was only a short street. At the corner with Augustenstrasse was the Café Heyde. A sewing and notions shop occupied the opposite corner and next to it was a furrier's, Pelzhaus Richard Haase, established 1695, owned by master furrier Richard Georg Haase, my father.

Family quarrels were the cause of great difficulties for my father. My grandfather had died young—I did not know him—and the fight over the inheritance ruined the once prosperous business at its original location. I was four years old when my father made a new beginning in Grüner Weg.

At that time we moved into an apartment at Paulstrasse. Where our street joined with Brandestrasse there was a small, well-kept triangular lawn, the *Dreieck*, with a low hedge of boxwood around it. I remember a telephone booth on the far side of the *Dreieck* and beyond it was the *Tonhalle*, a restaurant with a beer bar and a one-lane bowling alley. From our apartment to my father's fur store, we had to walk only down the street to the pharmacy at the corner, turn right on Augustenstrasse, cross over to Café Heyde and already we were in Grüner Weg, a matter of less than five minutes.

I have no idea why this short street was called Grün; there was nothing green there. Both sides were lined with shops and stores of many kinds. Near the far end was the delicatessen of Max Müller where my mother liked to shop. In the evening hours Grüner Weg was the liveliest. The narrow sidewalks were crowded with shoppers to get

1

quickly, before closing time at seven, what was needed for supper. It was a safe, middle-class neighborhood.

Sometimes I visited my father at the store. In the back, two steps down, was the workshop. My dad, with a cigarette in his mouth, always took such short breaths, opening his lips a little on both sides of the cigarette. I heard him suck in the air, a sound like my bicycle pump made when I pumped up a tire. Usually he was sitting on one of the high stools in his white smock, bent over his work. I watched him sorting out the skins, cutting and shaping them, or making templates. The front of his smock was always stained a bluish black from the dye in the furs. Sometimes I found him bent over on his chair; he always had such stomachaches.

It was dark and gloomy in the workshop. Only one lamp spread light wherever my father happened to be working. That made his face often look so pale gray. But in front, in the salesroom, it was bright. Light came in through the two large showroom windows, with the entrance between them. Besides, there were many lamps in the ceiling. When the door opened, a bell rang. Then my father changed into a clean white smock and came up the two steps to greet his customer. When we came—my mother, my brother or I—we always yelled right from the door, "Ich bin's!" so that my father wouldn't have to interrupt his work.

Today it seems to me, my life began with our move into the apartment at Paulstrasse. Running through the house, I slipped on the stone steps from the basement into the garden, which resulted in a bloody nose—an insignificant incident, but the earliest in my memory. Our spacious apartment was on the first floor, a half-story above street level. From the massive oaken main door a short, wide stairway led to the double-wing door, which opened to our entrance hall. We had bright, large rooms with high ceilings. Dining room and salon were towards the front. My parent's bedroom, with a verandah attached to it, and the bedroom my brother and I shared, were in the back. An outside staircase led from the verandah down into the garden. The bathroom could be reached from both bedrooms. An internal staircase ran from the hall to the lower level where our enormous, black and white tiled kitchen was located. Besides storage rooms, coal and potato cellar, the laundry room with the big wood-burning cauldron in the middle, the basement contained a small two-room apartment, which we rented out.

In the long and narrow garden we had a big spruce and a walnut tree, as well as raspberry, blackberry and gooseberry bushes. My father once tried to cultivate strawberries and my brother, Dieter, and I had to get horse manure from the nearby stables of the riding school. In the back where the garden made a little turn to the right, was room for a table and a few chairs. My brother and I each had a small parcel to grow flowers or plants of our choosing. Dieter made an attempt at some complicated plants; they didn't take. I sowed *kalendula officinalis*; they grew like weeds.

Above us lived Herr Brunnemann, our landlord, and his wife. Their apartment was the same size as ours, without the lower level, of course. The Brunnemanns were a very nice, couple. They were older than my parents and had no children. We celebrated holidays and other occasions together. Frau Brunnemann was especially fond of us children.

*   *   *   *   *

In those early years of my memory, I saw my father occasionally in Brownshirt, britches and boots. Sometimes, in the evenings, he went to meetings and occasionally there were fights in the streets, which I did not understand.

When I was six, my mother took me to the St. Georg Schule. I don't remember much of my elementary school years, except that I was not a good student. As I was to enter high school at age ten, I didn't pass the entrance exam. Only after my mother had a talk with my elementary school teacher, he gave me a better report card and I was admitted to Blücher Schule where Dieter was already in his third year. My mother had great powers of persuasion.

During my second year in high school I got sick. It wasn't like having pain or a raging fever, a rash or something like that. I was just sluggish, without appetite, weakly and my temperature was a little high. My mother went with me to the hospital to have me checked out. The doctors came up with something they gave a medical name I couldn't understand and sent me home, telling my mother I had to rest, stay in bed and take some pills. I thought, they don't know what I have; so they just say, stay in bed and take some pills. I think this went on for a month or so. My mother cooked for me all the meals I liked and a family friend brought armfuls of vegetables from her garden and after a while I got better.

Instead of going back to school, my parents sent me for six weeks to a children's home in the Black Forest. Oh, how I hated it! I was so homesick. All I wanted was to go back to Rostock. At the end of my long ordeal, my parents thought it would be nice for me to interrupt the long train ride in Berlin. A school friend of my mother's, a total stranger to me, received me at the train station and took me to her home in Zehlendorf, one of the better sections of the city. The following day her husband took their children and me in their car for a sightseeing tour. I had to see Unter den Linden, Kurfürsten Damm and the Reichstag, the German Parliament

Building, while all I wanted was to be back in Rostock.

The summer vacations were over when at last I came home. I was healthy again and I could go back to school. Everything seemed to be normal. There were no more street fights since Hitler had become Chancellor and nobody was without work or on welfare. People said they could be proud again to be Germans. The military was strong again, stronger than ever. Alsace and Lorraine returned to the Reich. Then the Wehrmacht occupied Austria and finally the Sudetenland and Czechoslovakia, Hitler's last, unopposed act of aggression. Germany became Gross-Deutschland, or the Thousand-Year Reich. Hitler had avenged the Dictate of Versailles.

But everything was not normal. I did not see my father wearing the Brownshirt anymore. The door to our store did not exhibit the sign with the Swastika. Citizens were discouraged from buying at any store that did not display the Nazi emblem. My father had Jewish friends, and Hitler did not like the Jews. Our business was boycotted. Once, as I was walking with my father, we met Herr Hirsch who was already wearing the big, yellow Star of David on his coat. My father greeted him, but Herr Hirsch said, "You better not do that anymore, Herr Haase, it is too dangerous for you!"

My father answered, "But you are my friend!"

I went with my father to the Bahnhof Hotel to see Herr Krischer and buy furs from him. He could no longer come to visit our store or have coffee with us at home. A few weeks later we heard that Herr Krischer had left Germany. I also never saw Herr Hirsch again.

One evening, on my bicycle, I followed the *Grüne Minna*, nickname for the police van, as it went from house to house along a street in the old part of town. The policemen dragged people out of their homes and shoved them into the van. I knew they were Jews, but I didn't know what they had done wrong. The next day the Synagogue in Augustenstrasse burned down and some villas in Schillerstrasse and Stephanstrasse were ransacked and plundered. Herr Hirsch used to live in Schillerstrasse, but he was no longer there.

Hitler made angry speeches on the radio. The Jews were to blame for everything. People were afraid to say what they thought, to talk to their neighbors, even their friends. Listening to the BBC was prohibited. There was talk of expansion to the East. Tension was in the air. People were nervous.

At about ten at night, on 27 August, 1939, our doorbell rang. My brother and I were in bed but not yet asleep. We heard the voice of a man we did not recognize. He left after only a minute. Somehow I knew something enormous had happened. I went into the living room where my parents stood talking. I remember crying and clinging to my father. He held in his hand a piece of paper the stranger had delivered. It was his draft notice.

The following morning I rode my bicycle to Ulmenstrasse. Some hundred men in civilian clothes with suitcases were being organized into groups on the grounds of the barracks. I did not see my father.

*   *   *   *   *

Our dining room had become also our living room. What we used to call the salon we had rented out to a young married couple, the Olaffs. That last year before the war must have been very hard for my father. Customers stayed away, afraid to be seen entering our store. It must have been hard for my mother, too, giving up a room of our apartment, but necessary for the extra income. Most of our daily lives took place in the dining room, around that big, round table in the middle. A long flat buffet stood against one wall and the sideboard—we called it the *Kredenz*—with precious china and vases, crystal and glasses on the other side. There was a grandfather clock in the corner next to the tall windows framed by heavy curtains. Above the buffet was a painting, a seascape. Ernst Heyde, a friend of the family, had painted it and gave it to my parents as an anniversary present. On the *Kredenz* stood a white porcelain angel, dancing on a golden ball.

Herr Olaff was a young lawyer in the legal department of the city's labor and employment office. Being new in town, in search for a place to live, he by chance met my father on the street and asked him where he could find Brandestrasse.

"What do you want there?" my father asked him, guessing his intention.

"Rent a room," Herr Olaff replied.

My father said, "You can do that at my place!"

The two men discovered right from the start that they had a common sense of humor. The Olaffs moved into our salon. My parents and the much younger couple became friends; my brother and I had much fun with them.

Then came the war. The Olaffs moved out; who knows where they went and what became of them. My father was now in the Wehrmacht and my mother saw herself burdened alone with the task of dissolving the business. In the first weeks and months she was fully occupied with sales, inventory, invoices, loan payments and bank credits. Besides, she

5

had to take care of the household. She was constantly running from the house to the store, to the post office, to the bank, to customers or suppliers and to see that we had food on the table. The years when we could afford a maid were far in the past.

People had forgotten that they should not buy at our store. They looked for opportunities to invest their money in valuable objects and bought silver, gold, jewelry and furs in a frenzy. My mother could hardly cope with the demands until she had sold the last piece of merchandise. All pending bills could be paid, all credit satisfied. When the final step to close the business came, my father had a one-week furlough to assist my mother. It was the end of the nearly two hundred fifty years old Pelzhaus Richard Haase, established in 1695.

Near Klühs, not far from Güstrow in Mecklenburg, was a munitions factory, well hidden in the woods. The company to which my father was assigned was stationed in Klühs for the protection of the Installation under the command of Hauptmann, Captain, Bründel.

On a Sunday, my mother, Dieter and I took the train to Güstrow and on to Klühs to visit my father. The billet used to be a country inn and tavern. Some of the soldiers were lying around on a thin layer of straw; others played cards or wrote letters. Cigarette smoke filled the room.

My father found a table and a couple of folding chairs and we unwrapped a hard salami, butter and a loaf of his favorite dark bread. His uniform was wrinkled and certainly not new. He looked pale. There wasn't much light in what seemed to be the dance hall of this former tavern. We watched while he ate and told us of his duties, his comrades and his free time. The food was not very good, he said, and we saw that the conditions in this billet were not very different from a homeless shelter.

He was off duty and we could go for a walk together. My father tried to be cheerful and it seemed a little easier for him outside. We walked through the small village and into the forest. It was a mild early fall day and it felt almost as if we were hiking in the *Heide*, the woods on the outskirts of Rostock, as we used to do in peacetime. We went as far as to a high wire fence that, my father explained, closed off the area surrounding the Installation. He said, on duty he had to patrol a length of some two kilometers inside the fence, walking back and force, carrying a rifle, for eight hours at a time. Dieter and I found that exiting, real soldier's stuff.

Hauptmann Bründel was a high school teacher at the Blücher Schule in civilian life and he was a Nazi. He and his family were neighbors of ours, a few houses away on Paulstrasse. I never had him as a teacher, but Dieter did and there had been an incident. Herr Bründel had accused my brother unjustly of cheating or lying and my mother went to the school to confront Bründel. He had to admit his error, but apparently never forgot the incident. As his superior, he made life miserable for my father. He singled him out for particularly hard and humiliating assignments.

My father suffered again from his stomachaches. The vindictive treatment by his company boss, the unhealthy living conditions and the bad food had their effect on him. By the time he had come home for a few days to close out the business, my dad was determined to get himself out of the clutches of his vengeful captain and applied for an officer's training course. He was accepted, a triumph over Hauptmann Bründel.

Our lives at home had adjusted to the new circumstances in the absence of my father. We actually lived more comfortably. There were no longer the worries about the failing business and the boycott the Nazis had imposed. The steady military pay gave my mother peace of mind. My father, too, was better off although the course was very demanding, both mentally and physically.

In September 1939, the Wehrmacht had overrun Poland in a matter of days. Great Britain and France declared war on Germany. Hitler continued with his angry, hateful speeches. German troops engaged in "clean-up" work in occupied Poland—whatever that meant. Hitler had finagled a pact of non-aggression with Stalin and we feared no further conflict in the East.

The spring of 1940 saw the beginning of the real fury of war. France fell and the Wehrmacht marched triumphantly into Paris. The air war, the Battle of Britain, was in full swing. Hitler was jubilant. The more enlightened, the wiser among the citizens, however, began to see trouble ahead, my aunt Tatta among them. "Wir siegen uns tot," we win ourselves to death, were her words—in confidence, when no outsider was listening. Arrests and disappearances became more frequent. My father was safe from further persecution by the Nazis while in the Wehrmacht, but the civilian population lived under the constant threat of being overheard making some thoughtless remark. It was also dangerous to tune the radio to a foreign station. Trucks with detecting devices cruised the streets sniffing out who was listening to forbidden broadcasts. Everyone was careful in conversations with strangers and, yes, with friends. There were cases of so-called friends, or even relatives, who had denounced someone. It was best to keep thoughts to oneself, one never knew who was listening.

My Parents, 1942

* * * * *

I joined the *Jungvolk*, the first step of the Hitler Youth, when I was twelve. It was obligatory to join at age ten; perhaps my mother had pulled some strings, or it was because I had been sick that my entrance was delayed. I was small for my age, but agile and fast. I looked good in the uniform: black shorts, brown shirt, neckerchief with leather knot and *Schiffchen,* the brimless cap. Our troop met Wednesday and Saturday afternoons in a somewhat neglected park near my home. I liked these mandatory gatherings for exercises, marching and singing.

The leaders, boys not much older than I, liked me and had chosen me for the *Stammschar*, a specialized, elite troop. Here again I was among the smallest, but it did not bother me. I usually got to do the things for which the bigger boys were not suited. I loved to play war games in the woods; I was the first to run in gym shorts through the snow in the *Rosengarten*; I was a hero when I got a bloody nose boxing; I was tossed high into the air from a tarp in a school gym so that I could see the ceiling beams from above. I belonged and it made me feel good. This was almost the same as being in the Boy Scouts, banned under the Nazis, except that there was some political propaganda thrown in. Our first obligation was obedience and loyalty to the *Führer*, defending the *Vaterland* to the death. Parents and family were secondary. We belonged to the state, the Nazi State, the Third Reich.

My father finished his course and became a lieutenant in the administrative branch of the Wehrmacht. The one and a half years of training involved both classroom and practical instructions. The final exams, comprised of oral, written and physical tests, were not easy. Work in the classroom and in the field had been demanding. His health had improved, but he was no athlete, never had been. What brought him through was sheer determination. Back to his unit under Bründel was no option for him. My father always admired the military, the discipline, the structure. He seemed to be born to be an officer in the *Prussian* military, not a furrier bent over furs in a half-dark workshop. His happiest years began the day he put on his officer's uniform, and it showed. He had become a different person, confident, proud and content. He had climbed a mountain and I was proud of him. We all were.

Our life at home had also changed. With the better pay families of officers received, my mother began to redecorate the home. The furniture in the salon were re-upholstered, the walls hung with new wallpaper. As far as wartime allowed, she bought herself new dresses, shoes and handbags and when my father came on leave, they went out to dinners or the opera. It must have been the best time of their lives.

9

The other side of the coin was that my mother had the burden of dealing alone with my brother and me. I don't think I was a problem, but Dieter, age fifteen, became somewhat rebellious. My mother allowed him to take classes in horseback riding. He developed great interest in horses and helped feeding and grooming them. Sometimes he stayed overnight with the horses. I remember that my mother was very pleased when she heard that Dieter had become friendly with a girl from the riding school, the daughter of Doctor Schwassmann, but then he turned more towards nature and the outdoors.

He befriended an old man at the harbor, known as T-Willem, who had an open motor launch, a kind of work barge with which he carried sand from the beach to construction sites. T-Willem, according to legend, had an accident in which a ton of coal dropped on his head when the crane under which he worked opened its chute at the wrong time. His speech was impaired, he stuttered. People said he had a metal plate in his skull.

T-Willem lived in the port section of town and Dieter spent much time at his home that he described as neat and cozy. My brother talked to us about the old man, his wife and son as if he liked that family better than his own. He begged my mother to let him go on an overnight trip with T-Willem to carry sand from the beach. My mother was reluctant. After all, T-Willem and his family were total strangers. She went to meet these people and was impressed by their warm hospitality, their genuine kindness and obvious fondness of Dieter. She let him go.

We were at an age when brothers kind of drift apart. Dieter now had friends his own age and I was excluded. Körling Meincke was considered a little wild and my mother had reasons to be concerned. Körling's father had an electro-machinery company and Dieter was seen in town driving the Meincke truck, without a license, of course. The two friends built a *Segelschlitten*, an ice-sailer. In strong winters the Warnow River froze, forming a flat expanse of smooth ice. One perfect day when the wind had driven all the snow from the ice and blew hard across the open surface, they allowed me to go with them. The rather primitive sled cut from shore to shore across the frozen Warnow at a terrific speed, scaring a few pedestrians and skaters half to death.

Dieter had joined the Yacht Club at that time and I was eager to become a member, too. I had just turned fourteen when I went with my friends Hanning Löscher and Otto Arndt to visit Commodore Edler von Görbitz in his villa on Richard-Wagner Strasse. The name Haase was well known—my father had been a member—and the old gentleman gave the three of us an application, without questions or sponsors. Dieter sailed with his friends, I sailed with mine. I don't think we ever sailed together.

10

With the year 1942 the war turned more serious for us at home. The first air raids on German cities had taken place, but still we could not imagine what such an attack would be like. One night, Lübeck suffered extensive destruction by British bombers. The war had come close to us and a few weeks after the attack on Lübeck, Rostock was hit hard. In four consecutive nights, April 25 to 28, 1942 the city was turned to ruins in smoke and ashes. In the third night of this series of air raids, Paulstrasse was among the targets and we, too, lost our home.

The events are fresh in my memory, as if they had happened yesterday. We did not take the attacks of the first two nights too seriously. My mother thought it more important for us children to get our sleep and stay in bed. However, we stood in our pajamas at the window, fascinated by the spectacle of the searchlights like long fingers criss-crossing the night sky and our *Flak* shooting random fire. We saw and heard the war taking place outside our window, just as I, when I was younger, had imagined spectators could watch the war in safety from behind a fence. My childish imagination had become reality.

Most interesting was the second night when we could actually see a bomber caught in the crossing searchlights, like a fly in a spider web. I even thought I saw bombs dropping from the plane through one of the fingers of light. We heard the drone of the enemy aircraft, the barking of our guns, the explosion of bombs and felt the ground trembling. Doors and windows rattled. The sky became red and the city disappeared in clouds of smoke and flying debris. That night, we experienced the terror of the war for the first time.

The following day classes were canceled. Throughout our town there was devastation from the two previous nights. Some fires were still burning, rubbish smoldering. The smell of fire was everywhere, debris littered the streets. The old part of town was widely destroyed. People were trapped in their cellars; many had been killed or hurt. Water pipes and gas lines were broken and people had drowned or suffocated in their houses. *"Wer plündert wird erschossen!"* Police warned looters would be shot. There was chaos and confusion, terror and fear, homelessness and mourning. Many left town. My mother also wanted to leave, but I was determined to remain at home, and so we all stayed.

When the sirens sounded in the third night, we all got up. We had seen how close the war had come. The Brunnemanns came down and we sat in our hall. My mother sat to my left, the Brunnemanns next to her. Dieter was facing me, sitting close to the entrance door. On my right, I had the stairs that led down to the lower level. We each had a small suitcase next to us. The rumbling started far away and came closer very quickly. As long as no trembling and shaking accompanied the noise, it was anti-aircraft fire, the big 10.5s, the 88s or the tak-tak-tak of the 20 millimeters. We knew how to distinguish between the sounds and felt it in our bones when bombs exploded. But this night all the sounds mixed and the earth trembled a lot more. *Were these heavier bombs? Were there more planes above us? Was there more of our Flak?*

I held on to the seat of my chair with both hands as the house shook. The doors flew open. My brother closed them. The lights went out and we were breathing mortar dust. In the general noise we did not hear the windows shatter. The doors burst open again and I feared I might fall down the stairs. Bombs exploded very close in short succession and then there was the cracking and splintering of wood, a tremendous chord of the piano above us—then nothing.

The explosion came a second later. The whole house seemed to lift and settle in an angle. My brother yelled something and in the dark we scrambled through the entrance where the door had been, down the wide stairs to street level. The huge main door had jammed, hanging crooked in its hinges. I squeezed through the narrow gap, but my suitcase was stuck. A bomb exploded nearby and the heavy door along with chunks of concrete fell inward. I was on the street. I think I only then opened my eyes as I ran along the street to seek shelter or assess the situation. The *Katholische Klinik* a few houses away was on fire top to bottom. Half of the house across the street where my friend Jürgen Zander lived was gone. I ran back and found that the others were just coming out from under the door; luckily, the way the door fell, a hollow space was left underneath and nobody was hurt. Herr Brunnemann was just saying to Dieter, *"Ich hab' den ganzen Laden noch auf der Brust!",* I have to get this off my chest. Later we laughed about that.

More bombs fell in the neighborhood. We searched for shelter. The restaurant *Tonhalle* across from the *Dreieck* was about to collapse. We ran into Brandestrasse as a low flying plane shot at us with machine guns. My mother later asked what the *kleine goldene Perlen*, the little golden pearls, were, referring to the sparks the shells made hitting the pavement. A bomb exploded near the intersection with St. Georg Strasse and threw us to the ground.

We crossed into Bismarkstrasse. The bombing stopped but the *Flak* still hammered away. We went into the villa of the old Brunnemanns. They were very old. A feeble, old couple, sitting by the window watching the spectacle of fireworks above the city. The flashes of exploding bombs, the burning debris flying through the air, the red night sky—it was all a performance of great beauty to them. They did not understand the horror.

The rumbling of guns and bombs stopped. Firestorms raged in various parts of the city. My brother and I went back to our house. Dieter climbed in across the front door and began to salvage what he could. He grabbed armfuls of clothes from the wardrobes and threw them on the slanted door. The bundles slid down; I picked them up and carried them to a place in Brandestrasse where they were safe from the fire that advanced from the Catholic Clinic. I made several trips and Dieter joined me when there was nothing more to retrieve from the house. We had to sort our stuff from the belongings of other people. Then we carried what was ours to the Brunnemann's house.

My brother went back to Paulstrasse one more time. He returned carrying the porcelain angel from the *Kredenz*, protected under his jacket, and gave it to my mother. Miraculously it had survived intact.

Dieter found on the street a carton containing three dozen eggs, unbelievably unbroken. My mother was afraid to keep the eggs because of the order that looters would be shot. There was the rumor that a young girl who had found a box of stockings was shot on the spot by police. Therefore, my mother took the eggs and gave most of them away among the helpless and homeless people on the street. At the Brunnemann's she opened a bottle of red Bordeaux, stirred the remaining eggs into the wine and we drank the concoction. "It will give us strength," she said.

The elderly couple still marveled at the fireworks of sparks and burning debris flying over the rooftops in the storm created by the fires. The old lady said: "You can take another bottle of wine with you when you go home."

"Mother, we have no home," said her son.

"Ahhh, yes it burned down," and after a while, "Take the feather beds when you go home."

"No, mother, our home is gone."

Later more of the same. It was no use explaining, they just could not understand.

In the morning eight or ten houses in Paulstrasse were smoldering, burned-out ruins. We planned our escape from the city. Herr and Frau Hilke, former customers and friends of my father's, owned a farm near Schwaan, a small rural town. We thought of them as our refuge and discovered that some trains were actually running. One was leaving in the afternoon with a stop at Schwaan. As we boarded the train, my brother was at first not allowed to leave the city; at seventeen he was old enough to help clearing streets of debris or digging for survivors in the rubble of destroyed houses. My mother used her powers of persuasion and the three of us got on the train.

Toward evening, each carrying a suitcase, the three of us reached the Hilkes' farm, exhausted and not yet fully aware of what had happened, what lay ahead of us. Frau Hilke welcomed us as refugees. Later that evening we had to sit around the *Volksempfaenger*, the little Nazi-approved radio, and listen to one of the *Führer*'s angry speeches (We knew the Hilkes were Nazi sympathizers.) I fell asleep.

13

That night Rostock suffered a fourth air raid. We stood in the farmyard and observed from the distance as our town was further destroyed. We saw the searchlights and the rounds of our *Flak* and we saw the sky turning red from new fires. But this time the British bombers also suffered great losses. Many of their planes were shot down.

Years later, I came across a poem written by the renowned Rostock author and poet, Theodor Jakobs. It was published in 1942 with the title *Rostock, Du Alte Stadt*. I translated the verses into English.

Rostock, You Old Town

Of fire and of smoke
You old town are weary.
Dust and ash like blankets
make tree and bush look dreary.

There are no gables standing,
Red brick has given way.
Lost and broken belongings
On the old pavements lay.

The steeples' burning flames
Were rising toward the stars.
The towers and the city gates
Are ruined deep with scars.

The bleeding crimson wounds
That took your countenance
Have turned you into ashes,
Beyond all cognizance.

Now you old town are tired
And yet, you are awake.
There is a blossom blooming
At the ancient wall near the lake.

And so, from your sad ruins
A new face will arise,
For in your living bosom
The old love never dies.

(By permission of Frau Margarete Block-Jakobs)

* * * * *

Before we lost our home to the bombs we lived a relatively peaceful life. My father was safe in the military, stationed in various locations, a supply unit or a vehicle distribution depot, but always far from any war action. The *Wehrmacht*, the non-political branches of the armed forces, unlike the *SS,* was not yet under the immediate control of the Nazi hierarchy, but rather under traditional military leadership.

In the winter of 1941-42, before the devastating attacks on our city, my brother was determined to build a *Segelschlitten,* like the one his friend Körling Meincke had. Well, it was war; he couldn't just go to a store and buy what he needed for that project. The material had to be *organisiert,* appropriated; in other words, it had to be stolen. Dieter knew where, when and how.

It was in January or February, on a very cold day, that he asked me to help him "organize" some lumber. By four in the afternoon it was completely dark. The city was blacked-out. We went to a large lumber and construction materials depot in the old part of town, near the harbor, and waited at a gate until it opened to let a locomotive enter. Dieter went alongside the locomotive and disappeared behind the closing gate.

I waited for a long time in the freezing temperature. When finally the gate reopened and the locomotive came out pulling some freight cars, my brother appeared, crouching under the heavy load of two long, thick planks. He saw that I was shivering and recommended me to stand in the steam coming from the engine to warm myself while the train stopped.

The gate closed, the train started again and walking next to it we carried on our shoulders the heavy planks. We then continued through the crooked, old streets in absolute darkness. The steam that had not warmed me at all froze my coat, which became as stiff as the boards we carried. At last we made it home and deposited the lumber behind the house under the spruce and the walnut tree.

My mother had cooked potato soup with chunks of beef in it. Dieter gave me his portion of the meat from his plate, his thanks for having been his accomplice in the crime—a serious crime indeed, committed during the hours of blackout and therefore severely punishable.

Perhaps I was not fully aware of this at the time, but my brother, three years older, must have known. Did he want that ice-sailer so much that he was willing to take such a risk? In the end, the thing was never built.

When in April our house, along with eight or ten others on Paulstrasse burned down, the lumber lay still in the backyard behind the pile of rubble that once was our home.

My father was on leave for Dieter's confirmation. It was a big party, about thirty people, family and close friends. My mother had our home renovated to her satisfaction for that occasion. She said, "Now it is the way I always wanted it." Two weeks later it was a heap of rubble behind a hollow, burned-out façade.

My father, who was stationed near Stettin had heard on the radio of the devastation of Rostock night after night. I remember he came to see us at the Hilke's farm, and together with my mother, he prepared a

16

detailed list of all we had lost. This later proved extremely helpful in the process of reclaiming funds from the government.

My brother's confirmation party
Onkel Heini front right, Hans Godow far left, Tatta, end of table, facing camera

Eventually we found a nice, large apartment in General-Litzmann Strasse, formerly Hermannstrasse, just around the corner from Paulstrasse. After a week or so at the Hilkes', we came back to Rostock and stayed at my grandmother's until we could move into the new apartment. It was on the first floor, had a big dining room and an even bigger living room toward the street. An elongated hall separated the front rooms from the kitchen, my parent's huge bedroom and the bathroom.

In the rear of the apartment was a suite of two rooms and another kitchen that we did not use and left empty. My brother and I had our room in the attic. Eventually we were able to furnish our new home with modern, albeit wartime furniture—a miracle that it was possible at all because everything was scarce.

My father was transferred to Rostock because of his stomach ulcer and he could live at home. He was in charge of a transport unit stationed at the same barracks where his military life had begun almost three years earlier.

While at my grandmother's, I needed to have my appendix removed. I awoke one morning with a sharp pain in my side. My mother hurried with me to the *Universitäts Klinik*. A doctor examined me for a few seconds and then nodded, "I'll take care of that first thing in the morning."

A young medical student, who had once tutored me in math, later came to my hospital bed and showed me the appendix floating in alcohol in a glass jar.

That happened just before the summer vacation. I missed ten days of school because of my appendix, and I had taken none of the exams. Not being a good student anyway, I was left back. Dieter was better in school than I, but not exactly an excellent student either. It was in these days that he announced he had decided to quit school and start as an apprentice at the *Neptun* shipyard. My parents were dismayed, but Dieter was determined. His goal was to become a shipbuilding engineer.

During the summer of 1942, I started sailing seriously. With my friends Hanning Löscher and Otto Arndt, I spent most of my time at the yacht club, sailing the popular sharpies. At the club, two of these open eighteen-footers were available for us and we spent time on the water whenever the weather and the dock master allowed. We also helped with the work at the boat yard and our entire vacations evolved in and around the club. Often we didn't even pay attention to the air raid warnings. Since the four nights in April, only one attack followed. That time the British bombers again suffered heavy losses.

Ignoring the end of summer vacation, I continued sailing. Every day I was out on the water with Hanning or Otto, or with Cord of the old Rostocker ship owner's family. He was Dieter's age and like my brother, he awaited his draft notice from the Navy. After my mother discovered that I was skipping school, I had to limit my activities to the weekends.

*   *   *   *   *

Reasonable people had come to realize that Germany could no longer win the war. The question was what the end would be like. This subject, however, could only be brought up in the most intimate circles, and in hushed voices. Hitler had invaded the Soviet Union and the advance in the east had broken down in the Russian winter of 1942/43. The air war over England became less and less effective. Rommel had to retreat in Africa. The front from Norway to the Balkan and the occupation of France and wide regions in the East drained the German economy and the Wehrmacht severely. Air attacks on German cities increased, especially in the industrial areas. Rostock suffered only sporadic and not very concentrated bombings, but that changed with the entrance of America into the war.

My father, my brother and myself in uniform.

News from the eastern front about retreats and defeats became more frequent and the numbers of casualties rose. The son of T-Willem, Dieter's friend, was reported killed in action near Leningrad. Almost every family suffered the loss of a loved one.

More often we heard rumors of arrests. Those who no longer believed in the *Endsieg*, the final victory, and did not hide their thoughts, suddenly disappeared. One day my dentist, Dr. Krüger, was gone, his practice closed. It was wise to ask no questions. There was talk of concentration camps, but nobody really knew what they were. Just having heard of *KZ* could land you in one of them.

Since 1943, I was in the *Marine Hitler-Jugend*, probably the least political branch of the Hitler Youth. The uniform was like that of the Navy but of course, with the swastika on the right sleeve. We had the trouser legs widened by sewing wedges into them to give them the bell-bottom look of the sailor pants. Hanning, Otto and I had more experience in seamanship than our leaders. In a three-week course I had passed maritime sport exams and I wore on my left sleeve the red anchor with two chevrons, among other insignia. Hanning had even earned three chevrons.

In October the boats had to come out of the water to be set up for winter storage. The three of us helped with the work in the yard, but in the evenings, especially in the winter, it was the custom for boys and girls—at least the more rebellious ones—to meet in Blutstrasse, one of the main shopping streets. We strolled up and down the narrow, crowded street with no real purpose. This was called the *Bummel*. Occasionally it came to minor fights between the true Hitler Youths and those opposed. Although my hair was too long and I wore the forbidden white scarf, I was never involved in a fight. The *Bummel* was the place where boys and girls met and, being fifteen, I had become interested in girls.

Dieter realized very soon that he had made a mistake leaving school and he asked my mother to plead with Director Freimann to readmit him. The principle made an exception. Dieter left the shipyard and returned to school. Freimann said later to my mother that he was very happy to have made that decision, for my brother became an excellent student.

He did not show up at the *Bummel*; perhaps at eighteen, he was already too old. He had become more serious about life and did not like my choice of friends, my hanging out on the *Bummel*. He told my mother about it. He also told her that in school I associated myself with the less desirable boys and with troublemakers. She reprimanded me but, really, my parents didn't have anything to worry about. I wasn't that bad and things remained pretty much the same.

Dieter was drafted the *Reichsdeutscher Arbeitsdienst*, the *RAD*. This Nazi Labor Column and its offshoot, the Todt Organisation, *OT*, built the West Wall, the defense line on Germany's border with France, the Autobahn and other projects in preparation for the war. Every young German served six months in the mandatory RAD before entering military service. I do not remember what Dieter's assignment was and saw him only once or twice in earthen-brown uniform with the jackboots and the swastika on the right sleeve.

Meanwhile, I continued in the Marine Hitler Youth, sailed in the summer and worked with the old caretaker at the yacht club in the winter. I had little interest in school and consequently my scholastic achievements were poor.

I was happy when our class was sent out to help on the farms with the harvest of potatoes and other crops. Most of the farmers were friendly towards us city kids; others, however, were demanding and unreasonable in the workload they gave us. We slept on straw in the worker's quarters or in barns and were generally fed well. Parents were glad to have their boys away from nightly air raids on the city, and with better food than they could provide.

At one particular farm the owner treated us very unfairly. We were eight or ten boys and slept in an upstairs room of the main building. In the early mornings, before daylight, we had to be out on the field, pick up the potatoes the machine had dug up from the freezing soil and carry them in baskets to a waiting truck, then run back, gather more potatoes before the machine came around again. Often the machine was too fast and we had to start a new row before we could finish the previous one.

We protested and the old farmer, whose sons were fighting in the war, roared at us. "You have to do your part in the war effort," he screamed. "Twelve-year-olds can do it, you just are too lazy," he rambled on.

That evening one of the older boys and I devised the plan for our escape during the night. We located a ladder in a shed. It was my idea to hide the key for the toilet downstairs, as if it had fallen out of the lock. We went to sleep in our straw filled room, leaving one guy awake to call us after midnight. At that time the two of us, shoes in hand, tiptoed downstairs. We crossed the hall next to the old man's bedroom and went out the main door into the yard. Had we been caught, we would have said we had to go to the bathroom but it was locked and the key wasn't there. We hurried to the shed, picked up the ladder and carried it to the window of our room. One by one the guys came down.

We had a long walk to the nearest train station, but by noontime we stood in the principal's office and reported to Director Freimann what had happened. He had some harsh words for us, but in his stern face I detected that he was more than a little amused by the story of our successful escape.

*　*　*　*　*

In January of 1944, my class was called up as *Luftwaffenhelfer* and assigned to the anti-aircraft unit stationed north of the city. There were the *Heinkelwerke*, the aircraft factory that produced the enormously successful *He 111* bombers.

I had been waiting for that moment: away from school, with a bunch of guys, out for adventure. Full of enthusiasm we boarded the truck in front of the school we shared with the high school girls, since the attacks in 1942 had destroyed our school. As auxiliary members of the *Luftwaffe*, our uniform was that of the airforce, but with the swastika on the sleeve. Most of us—I of course among them—removed the armband, which set us apart from the air force. We wanted to be soldiers, not Hitler Youth.

Our weapon was the 4-barrel 20 mm anti-aircraft gun. Seven personnel manned these weapons. For several weeks we were instructed in our respective duties. I was assigned the job of handing the gunner the loaded magazines and receive the empty ones. Precise and accurate movements were essential. In this teamwork we had to be familiar with our jobs in the dark as well as in daylight. I also had to operate the secret electronic viewfinder and learned only how to work it, not how it worked.

We practiced with blanks. As long as I was there, which was only about two months, we never fired a shot with live ammunition. The British aircraft came in at night at altitudes our guns could not reach and the fast *Mosquitoes* came in flying so low, we would have hit the hangars of the Heinkel Works instead of the planes. The American bombers approached by day in waves of hundreds of planes. Flying in over the Baltic Sea, they headed south to Berlin. At heights of ten thousand meters they looked like silverfish and were out of range even for the bigger guns.

Our instructions included identification of our own and enemy aircraft. We also had to learn to distinguish ranks and how to address an officer. In one class, when asked how to address the *Führer*, I said in a low voice, "*Gefreiter*" (corporal, Hitler's rank in World War I). The instructor had heard me. He called me aside and said, "What we privately think is our business, but in future you better keep your remarks to yourself." I could have been in deep trouble. (The correct way to address Hitler was, of course, *Mein Führer*.)

We lived in wooden barracks, with the wind blowing through the cracks. Some mornings I found snow on my blanket. The little wood-burning stove did little to keep us warm.

As I said before, I never fired a shot. That was okay with me. I was there for the camaraderie and I enjoyed being one of the guys. In the evenings we played cards, told stories, ate food we got from home and smoked (although that was against he rules—we were still kids). Often our sergeant joined us; he was young himself and seemed to like our company. Bedtime for us youngsters was strictly observed. After nightly air raids we were allowed one additional hour of sleep. The regular soldiers received extra rations of cigarettes. Every weekend a few of us were on leave either Saturday or Sunday, but at night we had to be back at our post.

Then, one day, out of the blue I received orders to report to the

Orthopedic Clinic in Rostock for an examination. I had no idea why this happened. From time to time I had complained of an occasional pain in my knees, but how this insignificant detail had become known to the superiors of my unit was a mystery to me. Nobody but my parents knew about it. Could my father, by that time a captain in the Wehrmacht, have done something? Could my persuasive mother have pulled some strings? How? And why? I was safer with the *Flak* than in the city where random air attacks had again become more frequent.

Anyway, the examination and x-rays from head to toe revealed that I had something they called *Scheuermann's* disease, which supposedly caused the minor discomfort in my knees.

Thus diagnosed, I had to lie for two months straight, day and night, in a cast of plaster while feeling perfectly healthy.

That was the reason for my time as *Luftwaffenhelfer* not lasting longer than a couple of months. Into the spring I stayed in my plaster shell, like a turtle turned on its back. My mother accommodated me on the new convertible sofa in the living room, under the big bay window. Only when the air raid sirens sounded did I leave my "mold". I dressed in minutes and walked up and down on the street in front of the house. Even on the day the *Neptun* shipyards were bombed and our *Flak* was shooting like crazy, I was too happy being outside and refused to go into the fortified basement shelter.

My mother cooked my favorite dishes for me, as far as the war rations allowed. She brought home a dog to keep me company, but the poor puppy, used to running free on a farm, caused all kinds of mischief in the house. My mother returned the animal that same day. Two girls from the yacht club came visiting, brought me a book by Louis Trenker, but I was too shy or too embarrassed being seen in that carapace, to receive and thank them properly.

My father was stationed in Rostock and because of his stomach ulcer he lived at home. At night, even before air raid warnings sounded, a driver picked him up when enemy aircraft approached.

Dieter had returned from the *Arbeitsdienst* and was waiting to be drafted into the Navy; he had applied for an officer training course. My mother learned window repair to show good will in the war effort.

Time passed slowly for me, but the day came when the x-rays showed that I was no longer required to stay in the "mold" twenty-four hours a day. Soon I also quit taking the required rest periods during the day, took the thing upstairs into my room and continued sleeping in it at night. It was springtime and I longed to be out on the water again.

In the morning of Sunday, 9 April, 1944 Rostock suffered a heavy attack by American Flying Fortresses. Hundreds of bombers approached in waves, each consisting of a number of *pulks,* formations of aircraft within a wave. They came in over the Baltic Sea and headed straight for Rostock. Alarm sounded and my mother, Dieter and I hurried to the big, new bunker at the main railway station. This bunker was five or six stories high with walls and ceilings of solid, reinforced concrete, several meters thick. In less than half an hour we heard the all-clear signal. The bombers continued east and it seemed Stettin would be the target. However, the planes turned around without dropping their bombs and headed again for Rostock.

We left the bunker and started for home, when the sirens sounded renewed alarm. In the meantime, two trains carrying soldiers on leave from the front had pulled into the station. The rooms and corridors in the bunker filled beyond capacity. The crowd shoved and pushed as more people tried to make it inside. In the confusion some ended up in the restricted areas still under construction.

Suddenly explosions drowned out the noise from the crowd of soldiers, women and children, all pressed close together. The bunker shook and rocked as bombs exploded above and on the side. The lights went out, we breathed dust of concrete and mortar. Men tried to get through with stretchers and medical kits to reach casualties in the restricted corridors where a steel door had blown in. This added to the general confusion. Emergency lights came on and the crowd began to move towards the stairs and exit. At length we reached the bottom. Outside, where the bicycles and baby carriages had been, we saw nothing but twisted metal. One bomb had hit the concrete wall high up near the top of the bunker, and another in front of the entrance. The damage to the structure itself was minimal.

On the way home we noticed little damage but, oddly enough, the villa opposite our house was a heap of bricks and splintered wood. Only one wall was still standing. The front of our house, facing the ruin, was peppered with holes in the plaster and the windows were gaping holes. We could hardly believe that the only house destroyed in our neighborhood was right in front of us. A stray bomb must have hit it.

My father was already in the apartment when we came in. He poured water into a smoldering hole in the couch. *How did that happen?* There was no fire anywhere. Perhaps a hot fragment of the bomb? *More likely, my father had let his cigarette drop from his mouth.* There were holes in the walls, a painting ripped to shreds, plaster, glass and debris everywhere. I went up into my room in the attic. There was a gaping hole where the window had been.

One night we slept in the damaged house, then my mother, my brother and I went by train to Lüneburg where we stayed at my grandmother's. A month later we moved back into our apartment in the provisionally repaired house.

Shortly thereafter, my brother received his notice from the Navy. He had been accepted for the officer's course.

*　*　*　*　*

When later that year the façades of the burned-out houses in Paulstrasse were taken down, I stood at the *Dreieck* and watched. With a long cable hooked into the holes that once were windows, a tractor pulled down what remained standing. After the dust settled, I climbed over the pile of bricks that had been our home and stood in the abandoned garden. The planks for the ice-sailer that Dieter and I had *organisiert* one cold winter night were still there.

Paulstrasse became an empty lot. Reusable bricks, cleaned of old mortar by Russian prisoners of war, served as valuable resource for reconstruction.

Our lives moved along with the events of the war. The war dictated our thinking, our actions, our fears and our hopes, our daily routines. Air raids had become part of that routine. Wave after wave of hundreds of planes flew in over the Baltic Sea, turned south near Rostock and bombarded Berlin. Now and then bombs fell on our city and another major attack could occur at any time.

This possibility did not deter my friends and me from sailing. In my memory, the weather in the spring and summer of 1944 was exceptionally beautiful. Every day I went out in one of our sharpies, usually with my friend Cord of the old Rostocker ship owner's family, who always brought a box of Greek tobacco for our pipes. (One of his father's merchant vessels had returned from the Mediterranean.) School was at best sporadic, constantly interrupted by air raid warnings, so I didn't go at all. I was certain to be kept back again, anyway. I had missed too many school days, first as *Luftwaffenhelfer,* then two months in the plaster mold and finally the two weeks we had spent in Lüneburg.

While my brother was still waiting for his acceptance to the officer's training course, he often went to see his old friend T-Willem, but he spent most of his time preparing for the *Abitur*, the high school diploma. However, his orders came before he was able to take the exams and he left for the Navy station on the North Sea island of Föhr. My parents were relieved: Dieter would not be in any immediate danger.

Before he left, my brother spoke once more to my mother about his concern for me, that I was not going to school, that I was hanging out with the wrong crowd, that I smoked, that my hair was too long and that I headed for trouble. I must admit, I was somewhat rebellious, but these were irregular times. My mother was lenient with me. My father spent

25

little time at home. Because of the frequent air raid warnings, he stayed more often at his post at the barracks.

After my discharge from the *Flak* and my two months in the cast, I did not rejoin the Hitler Youth. I never attended another meeting, pretending I was still sick. I had been seen on the street, however, and ordered to do messenger duty at the shelter of the *Hotel Nordland* during air raids. If I remember correctly, I went there only once. I felt very stupid sitting in my uniform among the hotel guests in the bomb shelter.

Word about my rebellious behavior got around to Hitler Youth headquarters. With my hair too long, smoking on the street and wearing the forbidden white scarf, I gave all the signs of dissension. Consequently, I got a rough haircut at the *Bann,* the Hitler Youth headquarters. My earned insignia were removed from my uniform sleeves. Thereafter I never again wore the stripped uniform blouse and pants, except for sailing.

*   *   *   *   *

My friend Jürgen Zander had lived diagonally across the street from us. Since the loss of our homes in Paulstrasse, we did not see each other often. He, with his mother and sister, had left Rostock the day before the fateful night in April, 1942. I don't think anybody was in the house when the bomb struck and tore down one side and most of the front.

The Zanders relocated to Gelbensande, half an hour's train ride east of the city. The Grand Duke of Mecklenburg had given up several rooms of his hunting castle to accommodate three families that had become homeless, and the Zanders were one of them. His father, Herr Zander, was not with them. I had never met him until much later. Jürgen never spoke of him, but my mother told me that he was a political prisoner. As a journalist he had worked with an underground publication in the early days of Hitler's rise to power.

Once I visited my friend for a week in "his castle". It was something special to live in a castle; we were always on discovery expeditions, especially in those parts of the castle that were out of bounds to us.

During one of our explorations in the attic, we heard Jürgen's mother and the caretaker come up the stairs. We found no better place to hide than in the big wicker hamper. As we were both inside with the lid closed, the two of them stood nearby, talking of all kinds of things. Occasionally they leaned against the hamper, making the wicker material creak, while we, squeezed inside, hardly dared breathing. After what seemed like an hour, we at last could come out, bathed in sweat. Jürgen's mother never found out about it.

26

Jürgen had an interest in chemistry. (Later in life he earned a doctorate in chemistry.) We experimented with liqueurs, using pure alcohol; concocted poisons; made baking powder, which his mother refused to use, and created explosives. Once we tried to blow up a tree. We had little success—it remained standing, only a little crooked.

One day during my stay at the castle, the Grand Duke came to see who was living in his castle. He was a very tall, slender and elegant man in his sixties. During his short visit, he greeted the three families who had become his tenants and I, too, was privileged to get a brief handshake. His Highness and his entourage then left promptly, presumably for his principle residence in Schwerin, the capital of the Land Mecklenburg.

*   *   *   *   *

Our apartment in General-Litzmann Strasse, formerly Hermannstrasse, had become too big for us. Dieter was no longer at home and I occupied the attic room. After the destructions of 1942 and 1944, there was a great shortage of housing in the city and we had the extra two rooms with a kitchen, a small apartment in itself, which we never used.

It was no sacrifice for us to give up those rooms and Major Ferdinand Kurth and his wife moved in. Major Kurth, promoted to *Oberst*, Colonel, had become the military commander of the city of Rostock, which had been declared a *Festung*, a fortress. He was an officer of the old school in the Prussian tradition. My father adored the ideal of Prussian militarism and my parents quickly became friends with Colonel Kurth and his wife. The Kurths were a refined, elegant couple. He had been severely wounded in the abdomen and was in constant pain, walking bent over, with the aid of a cane. He carried several decorations pinned to his impeccable uniform and always had a smile on his finely chiseled, emaciated face.

During the summer of 1944 the eastern front drew steadily closer and already approached the borders of the *Reich*. An endless stream of refugees moved westward by road and by rail and, as summer turned into fall, people fleeing ahead of the advancing Red Army crowded into town with horse-drawn wagons and on foot with pushcarts. Many of them were too weak to go on and they stayed. Soon all emergency shelters, schools, churches and public buildings, were filled with refugees.

Overcrowded trains came through Rostock packed with people who had been underway for weeks. Often trains with their human cargo remained standing for days at the main railroad station or on open stretches of the tracks. The conditions in those rail cars were horrible, without the most basic sanitary facilities. Old people died and children were born in them.

The Hitler Youth was sent in to give assistance in what was an impossible situation. I went once to the *Hauptbahnhof*, the main railroad station, and into one of these trains. I had no idea what to do or how to make myself useful. There were old women and young girls, small children and babies and a few old men, crates, battered suitcases, bundles—and a terrible stench. I pushed myself through a few cars and then I had seen enough of the misery without being able to do anything helpful.

I talked to two young girls from Königsberg, later Kaliningrad, and learned they had been on the train for six weeks. One of them I met later in the city and she told me they had decided to end their ordeal and stay in Rostock. She looked very nice in a pretty dress, part of former riches. Her blond hair was cut stylishly short. I saw her several times before the Soviet troops closed in on the city and assumed she and her family then continued on their flight west.

Germany was losing the war. There was no longer any doubt about it. To say so openly, however, had become more dangerous than ever. Propaganda Minister Göbbels proclaimed with great enthusiasm that the *Endsieg*, the final victory, would be ours. He continued to promise the development of a mysterious new weapon and we could not fail. Did anyone really still believe that?

On all sides the front was on Germany's borders. Our cities, especially Berlin, were now under constant attack from the air. Food and materials were sharply rationed and in short supply. My mother visited the Klingenbergs, former customers of my father's, who had a dairy shop and she sometimes brought home some butter, milk or cheese. What she did was dangerous and could easily land her in jail. Once she tripped and fell crossing a street with a package of butter under her coat. For fear of spilling the butter on the pavement, she held her coat together and scraped her knees bloody for not using her hands to soften the fall.

My mother did everything she could to put food on the table, which became increasingly difficult. My father took his meals at the barracks where his unit was stationed. Somehow, we came in possession of a bucket of molasses, which we used for baking, instead of sugar. I learned to make *Honigkuchen*, syrup cake, which I took on my daily sailing trips, along with potato salad, and sometimes a fried herring.

Early October the boats came out of the water for winter storage.

The war had lasted five years. How much longer could this madness go on? Our wonder weapons, the *V 1* and the more sophisticated *V 2*, were pounding London. *With that we are supposed to win the war?*

The *Volkssturm* was established, units consisting of invalids, old men and young boys. There weren't even enough weapons for everyone to get a rifle or a *Panzerfaust*, the tank buster. The Nazis and the Hitler Youth formed partisan cells under the code name *Wehrwolf*, to do sabotage behind enemy lines.

We received the news that my brother was transferred from the Navy officer course to the infantry and soon thereafter we learned that he was deployed to the eastern front.

My father received his marching orders for Norway.

My mother and I were alone. Colonel Kurth and his wife were like family to us. It gave us a sense of security to have the Commander of the *Fortress* Rostock living with us; I was even a little proud.

A new winter was near. *Would it get very cold this year? Would the Baltic freeze as it did in the winter of 1940/41?* I remember climbing all over the mountains of ice that had accumulated along the beach. People could actually walk all the way across the ice to Denmark. In that winter my brother and I had used our sled to bring home coal for heating from the harbor. Would there be any coal at all this year? Nobody had thought that the war could last as long as it already had. We were waiting for the end, but we did not know what the end would be like. We could hardly imagine a life without air raids, without food rationing, without fear.

Dieter was now somewhere in Hungary, my father safe in Norway. He was so disappointed when the attempt on Hitler's life in July had failed. The war could have ended then and there. Instead, it went on, senselessly, and Soviet troops were already in Pomerania.

* * * * *

We followed closely the advance of the Allied forces in the West, but for us it was far more important to observe the developments in the East. While the American and the British forces approached the Rhine, aiming for the industrial regions along the Ruhr, they were at far greater distance from Rostock than the Soviets. If we had to be overrun, we wanted it to be by the British or the Americans, but that seemed increasingly unlikely. So many horror stories of atrocities committed by the "hordes from the East" were reported, the population was in fear. Refugees told of raping, looting and burning. We did not know how much of this was rumors or Nazi propaganda, and how much was true.

My father did not want to take any chances. Before he left for Norway, he asked Colonel Kurth if he could arrange to get us out of Rostock before the Soviets arrived. The city was supposed to be

29

defended and the population would be exposed first to the fighting and then to the uncertain fate under the occupation by the Red Army. Colonel Kurth promised my father to send us westward to safety.

The boats had come out of the water and I helped with the work at the yard whenever I could.

Every time I went to the yacht club, crossing the Warnow on the old steam ferry, I left behind the gloomy atmosphere that permeated the house. The fear about Dieter's safety and the worries about the future overshadowed everything. My mother was always afraid that someday the woman, whose ominous duty it was to bring the bad news of war casualties to the families, would ring our doorbell.

Also, the anxiety over my failure at school left me as soon as I arrived at the boat yard. With sailing suspended for the winter, I had returned to school, but classes were irregular and constantly interrupted by air raid warnings. Classrooms were not heated for lack of coal; we had to keep our coats on. My scholastic achievements were at best mediocre; only in Latin and English did I achieve passing grades.

In much of my spare time I worked on boats in the big shed at the yacht club, but in the evenings I met with my friends on the *Bummel*. I had a girlfriend. Marianne, not one of the most popular girls, was attractive with dark eyes and black hair and she dressed more fashionably than the other girls. However, I did not consider her "Yacht Club material", and only once did I take her with me across the Warnow to show her where I spent most of my free time.

My mother's fear had become reality. The woman who handed out the dreaded news in our neighborhood came to the house. I was not at home at the time, so I can only imagine the shock my mother must have felt when she answered the doorbell. The woman gave her a letter that had come from my brother's superior. She said, "Please read it, Frau Haase. I don't think it is so bad." And it wasn't. Dieter had been ambushed while on a reconnaissance mission behind enemy lines and had been taken prisoner. The letter stated, "...through no fault of his and while bravely executing his duty."

After the first shock had worn off, we had mixed feeling about Dieter's fate. On the one hand, the war was over for him; on the other, he was in the hands of the Russians. We would have been relieved had the Americans or the British captured him. But the Russians? The Soviet Union did not adhere to the regulations of the Geneva Conference. How would he be treated? Would he be sheltered, fed and provided with medical care if needed? Was he perhaps wounded? The letter had not mentioned anything about that. Would he be allowed to write? Could the Red Cross get involved? Would he be released as soon as the war was over?

We clung to the thought that he was alive. The Kurths were of great comfort to my mother. I had just turned seventeen. Too concerned with myself, growing up in adverse and insecure circumstances, I was probably of little help in this difficult time.

In Dieter's last letter from the front, he had written that he was "ninety kilometers south of a big city and near water that came from Germany." We interpreted the big city as Budapest and the water from Germany as the Danube. With that we had an idea where he had been captured, but where might he be now?

Work in preparation for the defense of Rostock against the advancing Red Army was in full swing. The fighting came closer and closer; we could hear the rumbling of the heavier guns. Forced labor, political prisoners, Russians and Poles erected tank traps in and around the city. They used anything they could find, from overturned streetcars, twisted steel beams and concrete blocks to railroad ties, radiators and furnaces of destroyed buildings.

Although it was obvious that the war was lost, the Propaganda Ministry continued to proclaim the *Endsieg* to be close at hand. Our cities were destroyed; the Wehrmacht was unable to stem the onslaught in east and west; fuel and ammunition reserves were exhausted; transportation was constantly interrupted and reinforcement non-existent. How could there still be talk of Final Victory? But, to say so was more dangerous than ever. The wife of General von Plessentin, prominent Rostock aristocracy, enjoyed an early spring day on the beach in Warnemünde. A passer-by suggested it might still be too cold for the beach. She answered, "Who knows if I can still go to the beach once the Russians are here!" Her arrest came promptly the next day.

Nobody could be trusted. Colonel Kurth gave us to understand, without clearly saying so, that he had no intention to defend our city. There were simply not enough resources, supplies and manpower to mount a defense. He was not willing to risk the lives of countless soldiers and civilians and cause more damage to Rostock in a senseless struggle.

I followed the development towards the end of the war closely and observed how the citizens prepared for the impending Soviet occupation. I thought of the promise Colonel Kurth had given my father. I desperately wanted to remain in Rostock, did not want to run away. I wanted to stay and not abandon my beloved wounded city, whatever might happen.

* * * * *

31

Heini Bartels and my father had been comrades in World War I and they had remained friends. My brother and I called him *Onkel Heini*. The son of a farmer, he had a small but sufficient income from the inherited land that he rented out. Onkel Heini did not need a job and, with nothing to do, he had joined the Nazi party and gradually climbed the ladder to a leading position.

He and his wife, *Tante Trude*, lived in a modified storage barn in the old part of town. They had converted the ground floor of the ancient building into a cozy apartment. Tante Trude was my godmother. She too was a Party member, and she held a position in the *NS Frauenschaft*, the Nazi Women's organization.

At the beginning of the war, Heini Bartels became the official overseeing the collection and recycling of scrap metal, paper and other reusable materials. As a high-ranking party member in the city, he had many privileges and, while ordinary citizens got thinner and thinner, he grew fat. His position entitled him to keep a private automobile, one of the few still around. My brother and I joked about his car always leaning to the left because of his weight. Whenever we met him, he was usually in his *SA* uniform. Both he and Tante Trude answered our *Guten Tag* emphatically with the official Nazi salutation of *Heil Hitler*.

Onkel Heini and Tante Trude had no children. They were genuinely fond of Dieter and me. When we were still young, we visited them sometimes in their home. We did that mainly because they always gave us five marks, a huge amount of money for us. They were both present at the party celebrating my brother's confirmation. Two years later, when we invited them to my confirmation, they declined. "Our political conviction is not compatible with attending celebrations of a religious nature," was their explanation. My father took it as a blatant insult and none of us ever spoke to them again.

This incident demonstrated what happened to countless families and friendships in Germany during the unfortunate years of the Third Reich.

The collection of raw materials was an important task for all citizens. The schools sent classes into the woods to gather herbs and seeds for use in the production of cooking oil, margarine and pharmaceutical products.

All this collecting and gathering was not my kind of fun. To reach my quota and bring the required minimum of beechnuts to school on a Monday morning, I once had to go alone into the woods on a weekend. Everybody had to take part in some sort of activity; everybody had to assist in the common cause.

The German people had to come together in the senseless effort to win a lost war and to make still more sacrifices and contributions. Volunteers solicited money on the busy streets for the *Winterhilfswerk*, the Winter Assistance Program, rattling red collection cans. I never knew where that money went. Maybe it lined Onkel Heini's pockets.

* * * * *

In the spring of 1945, when the rumbling of the guns from the front had become louder and almost uninterrupted, a letter from Party headquarters notified me to report to work on the defense installations in the Barnsdorfer Woods, just outside the city. My mother did not want me to go and do heavy physical labor because of my back and Colonel Kurth agreed with her. "But," he said to me, "then you have to get out of here immediately or you face arrest."

The Party, not the Hitler Youth, organized defense labor; to refuse such an order was a serious offense.

We had to prepare to leave the city, more to escape the wrath of the Nazis than the impending arrival of the Red Army. We had heard of deserters, German soldiers hanged on trees. In spite of such warnings I was not about to dig trenches or set up tank traps, neither did I want to leave Rostock.

I asked Colonel Kurth to request me for duties as messenger. "I am seventeen; others my age are at the front!" I said to him. He was not a Rostocker, did not know the city well enough to determine where fighting was taking place, where to send reinforcements, where counter attack was possible, where to order retreat. "My knowledge of the city would be invaluable to you. Let me stay in Rostock, don't send me away!" I pleaded. Under his protection I hoped to be safe from the Nazis.

His answer was firm. "I have made a promise to your father."

* * * * *

Warnemünde, the quaint fishing village of old, was also a modern resort town with a wide beach of fine, white sand on the Baltic Sea coast. It had been incorporated in Seestadt Rostock, the Hanseatic city on the Baltic Sea less than twelve miles inland on the river Warnow. *Tatta,* my father's aunt, my grandaunt, lived in Warnemünde. She had always lived in Warnemünde, as far as I was aware. She was called Tante Franz before I, as a toddler, changed Tante to Tatta.

Tatta was our refuge, our haven. In the summers before the war, we spend many Sundays on the beach. For lunch she always had

Brathähnchen for us, little broiled roosters, a treat to look forward to the whole week. *Brathähnchen* were her only specialty; never married, the kitchen held little interest for her. In the afternoons she came with us as we went back to the beach and she sat in a wicker *Strandkorb,* the roofed beach chair so typical on the Baltic beaches. My mother and father, Dieter and I built sand castles, swam and played in the sea. My father could not swim, but my mother loved it. In the evenings, sun-drenched and tired, we boarded the train for the half-hour ride back to Rostock.

Sometimes I stayed for a whole week with Tatta. Warnemünder boys did not go to the beach; that was for the tourists. I wanted to be a Warnemünder boy and went to swim with them in the *Strom,* a side arm of the Warnow.

On the Sundays before Christmas, my brother and I went by bus to Warnemünde. We worked on the Christmas gifts for our parents, noisily hammering, sawing, drilling and painting. The radio played Christmas music at full volume; the canary *Jeremias* sang and Tatta snored loudly, napping on the sofa. Before taking the bus back to Rostock in the evenings, we had baked apples with sugar and cinnamon.

The four Sundays of Advent my father kept his store open and, after closing time, he and my mother picked us up at the bus stop. If business had been good, we went for dinner at a restaurant.

In peacetime, we often went hiking in the *Rostocker Heide.* Tatta, who had been a teacher in the elementary school of Warnemünde, taught us about the trees and plants, the berries and the beetles. Back at her cozy home, she read to us from the books written in *Plattdeutsch,* the regional language.

She was an integral part of our lives, perhaps the central point. During the war, Tatta was an island of peace. My mother often rushed to her whenever she felt lonely or in need of consolation. She always returned calmer and more confident.

Shortly before the war, Tatta, at the age of seventy-five, went to America on board the liner *Deutschland.* Her nephew had invited her to a visit in New York. As soon as the war broke out in September, she looked for ways to return to Germany. Being a patriot, she did not want to be away from home while her country was at war.

She returned via Italy on one of the last passenger ship to cross the Atlantic in 1940 and she fascinated all of us talking enthusiastically about America. Some of her stories were certainly exaggerated, for she was a great storyteller.

When early in the war report after report of won battles came over the radio, Tatta was among the first to be skeptical. *"Wir siegen uns tot,"* she used to say. We will perish winning battles. Five years into the war we all knew she had been right from the start.

It had taken five and a half years to bring Hitler's Germany to her knees. We were in the final phase of the struggle and the end was in sight. From their bunker in Berlin, Hitler and his *Propaganda Minister*, Joseph Göbbels, continued to call for the heroic defense of the fatherland, while fourteen- and fifteen-year old children were fighting in the streets with hand grenades and rifles against Soviet tanks. They had long run out of heavy guns and anti-tank weapons. Still we heard, like a broken record, "The wonder weapon will secure the final victory for the *Grossdeutsche Reich!*"

* * * * *

I already mentioned the Klingenbergs. They had the dairy shop where my mother was able to sometimes get milk or butter for us. The Klingenberg's son, as a young lieutenant early in the war with Soviet Russia, had taken the Hungarian capital, Budapest, with only seven men. He had received the *Ritterkreuz*, at the time the highest decoration, for his extraordinary bravery. The principal of my high school, the *Blücher Schule,* had invited him, a former student, to speak about his incredible achievement. We were proud of our Rostocker hero.

There were many heroes and acts of heroism, but they could no longer win the war. Fierce battles were raging in Berlin. In some places of Germany's midsection, the Americans and the Russians had already met. The Red Army was approaching fast and presumed to reach the outskirts of Rostock in a matter of days.

The clubhouse and the grounds of our yacht club were neglected, the docks falling apart. The varnish on the boats deteriorated. The acid of the artificial fog used to hide the city from view from the sky, destroyed sails, rope and paint. Nevertheless, very early for the season and ignoring the impending doom, Hanning Löscher and I got one of our sharpies ready and into the water.

A Wehrmacht truck passed through Rostock on the way to the front to retrieve some secret materials. Colonel Kurth ordered the driver to stop on his return trip in Rostock in front of the number 12 General-Litzmann Strasse, before continuing westward.

The truck was expected on 27 April. That day Hanning and I went sailing. It was the last time I sailed on our river, the Warnow.

I came home late in the afternoon. Already from a distance I saw the truck. Colonel Kurth and his wife, my mother, the driver and another soldier stood in the middle of the street. I came up to them and I knew that for me life, as I knew it, was over.

I did not know how long they had been waiting for me, but I was aware of the distress I had caused my mother, how irresponsibly I had acted and how difficult I had made it for Colonel Kurth to keep the promise he gave my father. How much longer could he have been able to retain that transport?

I had refused to leave Rostock as long as I could, but now it was over. I hated running away, like a coward, leaving my friends behind.

Without letting me go upstairs one last time, I was ordered into the back of the truck. Our bags and bundles and cartons, bedding and clothing, piled on top of crates with army markings, left little room for my mother and me under the awning. My pants were still wet from the water of the Warnow.

We drove off. It was dark before we reached Warnemünde to pick up Tatta. My mother would not leave her behind. The truck was refueled at the airfield north of the Heinkel hangars and then we were on our way west. I had not said a word since they had forced me into the truck.

*   *   *   *   *

To leave everything behind, to lose everything again within a couple of years, must certainly have been hard for my mother. But I was concerned with myself. I felt as if the world had come crashing down. I was running away, deserting my town as the enemy stood at the gates.

Tatta was also very unhappy, ripped from her cozy home, but my mother had persuaded her to come with us. She was eighty-one years old. We helped her into the truck and tried to make her as comfortable as that was possible among the boxes and bags and bundles. She was a part of Warnemünde, and Warnemünde was a part of her. The foghorn at night, the sea gulls screaming on the fishing piers and the *mucke-picke, mucke-picke* sound of the fishing boats early in the morning as they went out to sea... How could she live anywhere else?

The truck rumbled along dark and poorly paved country roads, avoiding the highways for better protection against air attacks. I felt powerless. I did not move, sitting on a crate and leaning my head against a bundle of clothes or bedding. My mind was in turmoil. *Hanning Löscher, with whom I had been sailing only a few hours ago, could have no idea where I was. My friend Jürgen Zander... Was he still in Gelbensande in the castle? Had the Russian tanks reached it yet? Would Colonel Kurth be able to oppose the orders and surrender the city without fighting? Could he avoid the blind rage of the Nazi bosses? Could he and his wife escape to safety? Would we be able to return to Rostock?*

My mother carried in her handbag a letter from Party headquarters, addressed to me. It was my summons to appear for a hearing on that very date, 27 April, 1945. My refusal to report to work on the defenses of the city had caught up with me. It was the most compelling reason for me to disappear.

On May 1, 1945, Rostock fell without resistance into the hands of the Soviet army.

PART TWO
A Taste of Peace

The overnight trip from Rostock had come to a halt in the early morning as a British Mosquito flew low over the ground and fired at some rail cars on a track not far from us. Our driver stopped the truck under a cluster of trees where we remained, hidden under the fresh spring foliage, until late afternoon. In the evening we continued to Lübeck.

A small room in the attic of a house on Falkenwiese became my abode. My mother, Tatta and I had arrived in the Hanseatic city of Lübeck, famous for Marzipan and The Buddenbrooks. The house belonged to a friend of our family, Tante Irma, as I called her since childhood. She had married and moved away from Rostock many years ago but remained one of my parent's closest friends. Recently widowed, she had the room we so desperately needed. Tatta and my mother found accommodations on the second floor of the apartment.

I was in a daze. Uncommunicative and dejected, gloomily contemplating my dire predicament, I climbed the stairs to the attic room assigned to me and flung myself on the mattress of the narrow bed. The city was still under blackout. There was no curtain on the single window and Tante Irma warned me not to turn on the light.

In the morning, after a dreamless sleep, I awoke to my strange surroundings. In my unchanged mood I stood in front of the washbasin, splashed cold water in my face and then crossed over to the window. Across the street there was a meadow, a few trees and a lake. I opened the window, leaned out and saw to the right a boathouse and a swimming facility with cabins and a diving platform. This should lift my spirits, I thought, but it only increased my desire to go back where I came from. This would only be temporary, I told myself.

I went down to the second floor. Tante Irma, my mother and Tatta stopped talking. "We have some oatmeal and milk—well, that powdered stuff—but no sugar." Tante Irma turned to me. "Our ration cards are useless. Yesterday they had nothing in the store."

"That's okay," I answered. "I'm not hungry." I found it difficult to be friendly, but then added, "Thank you, anyway. I am going out, take a look around."

"Be careful," my mother said. "We are under constant air raid warning. They don't even sound the alarm anymore."

"The British will be here tomorrow or the day after," Tante Irma added. "I heard they are not going to defend the city. They'll just hand it over. But you never know, there might be some shooting."

I hope so, better than nothing. I can't take this calm. Nothing's happening, can't even hear the guns in the distance, like in Rostock. I went out.

I found myself walking along the lake that turned out to be a river. *An der Wakenitz* said a sign. A side arm of the Trave… was this to be a substitute for the Warnow I had left behind? I crossed a bridge and entered the inner part of the city. Old, narrow streets, cobblestones, ancient houses, precious gables. Kind of like Rostock, but not as nice.

Some of the churches had lost their steeples in the air attack of April, 1942. I came to a square market place, the picturesque *Rathaus*, City Hall, and the post office in red brick. Streetcars screeched in sharp turns. Hardly any ruins. I walked on. Another bridge. The Trave. A narrow river with a few old ships at dock. *Puny harbor, I can spit to the other side. Nothing like my wide, ample Warnow.* I strolled along on cobblestones past storehouses and old Patrician buildings facing the meager river. And again a bridge. The core of old Lübeck seemed to be surrounded by water.

The following days I continued to explore this city. While the inner city, the old part of town, resembled Rostock, *but not as nice,* Lübeck was larger with a population of around 165,000. There had been only one air raid on Lübeck and the only damages I found were the empty, burned-out shells of the ancient churches. Housing shortage was not as great as in Rostock, until the endless columns of refugees from East Prussia and Pomerania reached Lübeck. Tens of thousands, fleeing ahead of the Red Army, crowded into the city hoping they escaped the onslaught of the Soviets.

A couple of days after our arrival in Lübeck, British tanks rolled into the city, crossed the bridges and were greeted with relief by the inhabitants. Not a single shot was fired.

My mother was on the telephone with Hans Godow, a family friend from Rostock. How he knew where to reach my mother was unknown to me. Hans Godow, Onkel Hans to me, had escaped from a British prisoner-of-war camp. He just finished explaining where he was hiding and asking for civilian clothes, when the phone went dead. The post office had been occupied and communications were cut.

With one of my brother's suits in a paper bag I set out to find Onkel Hans. Tante Irma had a street map of the city and I located Kleine Bäckergrube near the old port. At one of the bridges I had to cross, an English soldier stopped me. All bridges were closed to civilian traffic. While he pretended to inspect the bag I was holding, he laughed and threatened me playfully with his rifle. Maybe he had forgotten the direction I came from, maybe he didn't care, but I was able to run away with the bag and I found Onkel Hans in a little grocery store, hiding in a back room, still in remnants of his military police uniform of the Wehrmacht.

Quickly he changed into the suit I brought. For the next several weeks he stayed with the friendly women at the store who were glad to have a man around the house.

Lübeck had fallen into the hands of the British occupation forces. Life normalized, but the shortages of food and everything else were severe. We had electricity for a few hours in the morning and at night. Gas was shut off permanently. We cooked on an open fire in the fireplace. There was no coal and we soon ran out of wood. My mother and I went into the woods at the outskirts of town, gathered what branches we could find and loaded them onto the cart we had borrowed from a neighbor. On subsequent trips we had to go deeper and deeper into the woods and soon there were no branches left. People began cutting down trees, which was under strict prohibition and serious punishment.

From time to time different food items became available. The occupation troops needed the storage facilities, or perishable goods had to be disposed of—whatever the reason, suddenly two pounds of cheese per person were called up on ration coupons marked for one hundred grams. We could eat cheese for days, but had no bread, no butter, no milk, no vegetables, no meat. Then each person got three pounds of raw, wet brown sugar. Nine pounds of that stuff, in a pillowcase, sat on the nightstand in my attic room. Hungry at night, I partook heavily of the syrup-like, sticky, smelly mess. Tante Irma had a great supply of saccharin, artificial sweetener; we didn't need the granulated molasses.

Then there were no more foodstuffs released to the population and we subsisted on the rations and poor quality ersatz products we could get in the stores. The warehouses were empty; the occupation army confiscated what supplies there had been.

Hitler and Josef Göbbels with his family committed suicide in the bunker in Berlin. Heinrich Himmler, chief of the Gestapo and the SS, killed himself with cyanide after capture in the Lüneburger Heide. Other leading Nazis were arrested and imprisoned, while many more disappeared, never to be found. Grand Admiral Dönitz, Hitler's successor, signed the unconditional surrender of all remaining German forces. The war had ended.

The first days and weeks in Lübeck were for me like a bad dream. I had no friends, nobody I knew, and I roamed the streets of an unknown town. The presence of British troops was not very noticeable. Sentries still patrolled the bridges, but citizens could pass freely in either direction. In the evenings I strolled along the Wakenitz and talked with soldiers, practicing my English. One of them was interested in my harmonica and I sold it to him for a pack of cigarettes—my first black market deal. I gave most of the cigarettes to my mother who took them into the gardens as barter for vegetables. Two cigarettes for a beet, three for a lettuce or a cabbage.

One evening I found a pocketknife, left behind by an angler trying his luck for a fish. Cleaned and polished, the knife looked like new. I went to the black market area in the downtown section near the port. This place had the appearance of a flea market. Unrestricted, and not secretive at all, people called out their treasures for sale, while others threaded their way through the crowd, looking for what they wanted or needed. From ration coupons to soap, from canned goods to utensils of any kind, from liquor to aspirin and tobacco—almost everything was available. The currency was the cigarette. Five poor-quality German *Sondermischung*, Special Blend, were the equivalent of two Players, Wild Woodbine or American Philip Morris. The better English cigarettes—Senior Service, Craven A or the likes—were more difficult to come by.

My pocketknife sold for a ten-pack of Wild Woodbine. I opened the pack and sold the individual cigarettes, making a profit. By evening I could buy two packs, but then I could no longer resist the temptation and smoked a couple myself. The rest my mother turned into cabbage and potatoes.

Tante Irma had a lot of those little packages containing saccharin. "Can you sell those on the Black Market?" She asked me. "Can you get bread and meat ration cards for them?"

"That should be no problem," I said. "Give me a couple of them. I'll see what I can get."

That stuff sold like hotcakes, for cigarettes, of course. Cigarettes, exchanged for ration coupons put many a decent meal on the table for all of us. I traded almost her entire supply of saccharin for valuable food stamps.

I took a brand new shaving brush that had belonged to Tante Irma's late husband to the black market. I was unsure how much to ask for it. A young man ripped the brush out of my hands and advertised it loudly. "A perfectly good brush! Finest quality! New! Never been used! Good for a lifetime! Forty marks!"

In no time at all I had a pack of Senior Service in my hands. "What else do you have to sell? Medical books? Instruments?"

"I have a microscope," I said, "but my aunt wouldn't let me take it down here." Tante Irma's husband had been a doctor.

"I want it. I'm studying to become a doctor."

The following day I brought the young man to Tante Irma. It was the beginning of a lively trade in medical instruments, books and an assortment of prescription drugs.

I spent most of my time on the black market at an intersection of narrow streets in the old part of town. Suddenly, one afternoon, the crowd disbursed. Some ran into side streets, others faded into doorways. Not sure what was happening, I made myself inconspicuous by entering a store that sold used clothes. Jeeps with military police drove into the intersection from all four streets at once, but there was nobody to arrest. Ordinary citizens went about their business in an orderly fashion. The soldiers, in helmets and with the MP armbands, stood around for a while. Then they got back into their Jeeps and drove off. Five minutes later the place was again crowded with sellers and buyers, as if nothing had happened.

This scenario repeated itself once or twice a week, a mere farce, not producing any changes. In spite of my interesting and lucrative occupation, I grew weary of it and became restless. I missed Rostock, my friends, the Bummel, the activities around the yacht club and the boat yard. *Would there be any sailing? What was the Russian occupation like*? There was no communication across the border between East and West. I wanted to know about the situation on the other side. Would it be possible to find a way into the Russian occupied zone?

I needed some diversion. Hamburg, only sixty kilometers away and in the same British zone, has always held a great fascination for me: a big city of two and a half million, Germany's most important overseas port; the Reeperbahn, perhaps the largest entertainment complex in the world; Hagenbecks Zoo; Planten Un' Blomen, the famous botanical garden. I had never been in Hamburg and had no idea how much of it had survived the ferocious air raids. Throughout the war, British and American bombers had targeted Hamburg more often than any other

German city, with the exception of Berlin. Entire districts were flattened, burned down, devastated.

I declared to my mother, "I'm going to Hamburg. Be back in two or three days."

"How will you get here? There are no trains, you know that. And what will you do there? Where will you stay?" My mother was beyond belief, but she knew, there was nothing she could do to hold me back.

"I don't know. I can't stay here. I'm going out of my mind. I have to do something."

I have no clear recollection of my Hamburg trip, except that I set out one morning, stood at the Autobahn for awhile, got a ride in a Mercedes *Kübelwagen*, the German version of a Jeep, driven by a one-armed man by the name of Sonnemann. I arrived in Blankenese, a posh suburb of Hamburg. In the home of Herr Sonnemann, a fancy villa overlooking the river Elbe, I got a glass of juice and then went on my way.

The events that followed remain a blur. I remember the Reeperbahn, dubious third-rate taverns, bordellos, cheap eating places, the subway, a park bench in Planten Un' Blomen, dance halls, scarcely dressed girls with excessive makeup. Contraband liquor, served in mugs disguised as tea, was too expensive for me. I drank Heissgetränk, an artificially flavored and colored syrupy drink. How did I get by? No idea. Faded blotches have diffused my memory. I never told anybody about those two or three days in Hamburg.

My return to Lübeck involved a lot of walking. From the last *S-Bahn* stop in the northeastern suburb of Ahrensburg I took to the road. I must have gotten a ride of some sort along the way, for I reached home in the evening of the same day I left Hamburg.

Hans Godow still lived at the grocery store in Kleine Bäckergrube, helping the women with chores better performed by a man: heavy lifting, unloading the delivery truck, stocking boxes and crates. In the evenings he also participated in the endless job of sorting ration coupons and pasting them on sheets of paper.

No longer in danger of being arrested for escaping from the POW camp, he sometimes came visiting us at Falkenwiese. The woman who owned the store had provided him with some shirts of her husband's who had not returned from Russia and was presumed captured or killed.

Onkel Hans was desperate to rejoin his family in Rostock. We had never heard of anyone who had crossed the *Grüne Grenze*, the border between east and west, in either direction. There were rumors of a wide corridor, the no-man's land, running along the frontier inside the Russian zone. To attempt crossing the Green Border would be suicide.

At length we discussed the prospect of going to Rostock. At first it was just a remote idea, farfetched, a wish we both had; little more than a dream. But then it became more and more a plan. Onkel Hans had good reason to try everything in his power to reunite with his wife and son. For me it was the adventure, the burning desire to make something happen, to end the boredom, but was it a reason to risk my life?

My mother listened to our discussions. She shook her head. "How can you even think about such nonsense? It's absurd! You get caught and that's the end of you. Can you even imagine what it would mean to me?" She implored me. "We still don't know if Dieter is all right, if they will ever let him come home. Think about that." She turned away and I knew she was crying. From the kitchen I heard her, "If only your father were here."

Tatta listened quietly. I understood where her thoughts went. She wanted to go too, but at her age... I knew she missed her home in Warnemünde terribly.

Food shortages escalated to levels at which the elderly could hardly survive. Children would have long-lasting effects from nutritional deficiencies. Those who had no access to the black market to supplement their caloric intake were indeed in peril of starvation.

Limited train service in the British and American zones brought some degree of normalcy back into the lives of the citizens. My mother made plans to visit grandmother in Lüneburg, southeast of Hamburg and also in the British zone. She anticipated a strenuous trip, with uncertain schedules and connections, in third class rail cars, or perhaps worse, in a freight car. Summer weather had settled over North-Germany and so at least an unheated train would not present a problem.

"I have to go," my mother announced. Grandmother was in her seventies and frail. "I hope I can visit Tante Lene and get some vegetables, eggs and maybe some meat." Tante Lene had a small farm near Lüneburg.

While my mother prepared for her journey to Lüneburg, Hans Godow and I seriously pursued the possibilities of crossing the Grüne Grenze into the Soviet zone.

Onkel Hans, my father's friend from the days when they were young, had escaped from the British POW camp because he was afraid he might be mistaken for SS, wearing military police uniform. Our hometown, Rostock, barely hundred-twenty kilometers east of Lübeck, was deep in the Russian Zone. He had a compelling reason to risk this dangerous border crossing into the territory from where no news, only rumors, had come since the Russians had sealed it off. No telephone, no mail, no rail or road traffic. Only rumors, and all bad. Rumors of rape and torture, arrests and disappearances, political interrogations, burning and looting.

Talk of people being sent to Siberia. Trying to cross the *Grüne Grenze* was lunacy. We never met anybody who had attempted it.

I didn't want to hear of such stories, of so much mystery. It was my firm resolve to return to Rostock; I never wanted to leave in the first place. When Onkel Hans turned up, our plans came together.

We bent our heads over the map of the region that seemed to us most ideal for our purpose, the Palinger Heide. Of course, we had no clue where the best or safest area would be for us to cross into the Russian-occupied territory. We just had to come to a decision and concentrated on the section closest to Lübeck, where the border was easy to reach. We took several trips by bus to Brandenbaum, eastern-most suburb of Lübeck, advanced into the woods, peered out from the last trees over the quiet, desolate, gloomy landscape before us. We committed to memory certain features like a tree here, a bush there or a slight rise in the flat, sandy terrain and took notes, even made little sketches. Never did we see a patrol or a sentry. The Palinger Heide seemed lifeless and unguarded.

What to wear and what to take with us was another matter of concern. Dark clothes, of course; a hat for my blond hair. I had an old briefcase that I could hang on a leather strap over my shoulder to have my arms free, for a minimum of clothes, socks, a shirt, underwear, half a loaf of dark bread and a knife to cut it with. My uncle had an army-gray canvas pouch from the Wehrmacht that he could fasten to his belt. He had burned his uniform and wore the suit my mother gave him. He had no other possessions.

In reality, our plans were naive. We had no experience, no advice, no knowledge how and for what to prepare ourselves.

And so we began our adventure one gray, dismal morning. It was early August 1945. We did not know what to expect, what dangers we were facing. Neither one of us had ever seen a Russian, and we had no clear comprehension what it would mean if we came face to face with one.

* * * * *

"Noch mehr Kamerad?" the soldier asked. He wanted to know if there were any more of us. He held his machine pistol, at the hip. Of short, stocky build, his face was blotched, bloated, and the eyes were narrow slots close under his khaki cap with the red star. Not taller than me, he was square and compact like a bull.

I answered him, "nein," and Onkel Hans said, "nein, keiner weiter."

45

No one else, and to himself he continued, "nix mehr Kamerad." He mumbled on, shaking his head, facing down, "Oh God, oh God". He was devastated, near tears, finished.

It was not more than ten minutes since we had come out of the trees, left the narrow path and stepped on to the yellow sand of the Palinger Heide. The sand was packed firmly under the light but steady drizzle and our steps were muffled as we hurried forward, crouching from one bush or low tree to the next. There was little vegetation on this sandy ground. I don't know why it is called Heide; there is no heather growing here. The few bushes seemed dead, dry and gnarled, their roots finding no nourishment. The even fewer trees refused to grow taller than six to eight feet.

It was absolutely quiet and there was no wind. Suddenly he was there, the Russian. We heard his hoarse voice the moment we saw him. He was definitely less surprised than we were. "Komm," he said and waved his weapon in the direction he wanted us to go. No more was said, only my uncle kept on mumbling to himself, hopeless and in despair, "Oh God, it's all over," hanging his head, not looking up.

We walked without hurrying, the Russian on our left, slightly behind, with his gun at the ready. We didn't see a threat in that and he showed no interest in the whole business. He was just doing his job.

We reached a slight elevation, closer to the woods we had left minutes earlier, before coming out on the Palinger Heide. Ordered to sit together, we leaned our backs against a larger tree that seemed to belong to the woods just a hundred yards to the West. And that's were the border was, along the edge of those trees. At least, we assumed that's where the border was. In those first weeks after the war the line between East and West was not yet clearly established. Only recently the Russian Zone had been extended close to Brandenbaum, Lübeck's easternmost suburb. Lübeck city buses had their last stop half a kilometer from the British border checkpoint. Beyond that, there was a narrow forest and then the Palinger Heide.

"Nicht sprechen! Sitzen!" One of the Russians growled at us. We had to sit and weren't allowed to talk. There were three or four Russians at this post. My uncle had stood up to have a look around. We tried to figure out if we were still in the general area we had surveyed from the edge of the woods before we started out. After the Russian had snapped at us we only whispered a few words now and then when none of the soldiers were near. One of them wore a belted khaki greatcoat; he had no weapon and seemed to be of higher rank. The others carried guns and wore Russian style tunics with baggy pants stuffed into the boots.

The steady drizzle had turned into a light rain. Our clothes had absorbed as much moisture as they could and we began to feel cold.

From time to time one or the other of the soldiers went away and usually returned bringing with him one or two people; sometimes even a small group, so that soon a dozen or more shared our fate. We all squatted on the wet, sandy soil, or sat on an exposed root of our solitary tree on the little hill, only slightly elevated from the rest of the dreary landscape. The prisoners were not allowed to stand up, but the Russians never sat down.

A man and a woman approached unaccompanied. They came directly towards us. The soldiers did not move. What was going on here? The two civilians had Red Cross insignias on their sleeves. The man—a doctor?—showed some papers to one of the Russians. They seemed to understand each other somehow, laughed together about something. The "doctor" pulled a stethoscope from his pocket, pretended to examine the Russian and they were having a lot of fun with that. Then the man took the arm of the young woman—a nurse?—and looking back, still laughing, they were on their way.

Now, that was a trick, if I ever saw one! And the stupid Russian went for it. *But, really: weren't we the stupid ones? Why didn't we think of something like that?* That couple just showed us how to do it right. We were angry and depressed. What would our future be like—if there even was a future for us?

After a while one of the Russians came up to us, looked Onkel Hans and me in the face, and then said to us and two other men, "Du, komm!" The four of us stood up. With his gun he motioned us to walk down the hill.

We felt uncertain about this and wondered what this might mean. We reached a dilapidated shed. The Russian kicked open the door that hung on only one hinge and said something we interpreted to mean, "get in."

I was very afraid at this point, but presently we understood what was going on. In one corner lay a pile of canvas tarp, and without words he indicated for us to load it on a cart, which stood just inside the door. The humid, mildewed and dirty material was hard to handle. At length we got it onto the cart and out the door. The other two men, both younger than Onkel Hans, pulled and we pushed. The Russian showed us the way without speaking. Maybe this one didn't speak any German, while most of his comrades seemed to know at least a few words. He also didn't help with the cart when it got stuck in a soft spot or when the wheels caught a bone-hard root sticking out of the sandy soil.

We came to a wooden hut, set deep in a dug out square with only the flat roof above ground. On three sides it was pretty close to the dirt walls, leaving only a foot or so of space, but on the fourth side where the entrance was, a wider space had been left open with a ramp leading down to the door. The Russian instructed us in sign language to cover the

47

hut with the tarp we had brought. The stiff and rough canvas was difficult to handle and it tore and chafed on the skin of our hands and broke the nails. But we got the job done. The canvas tarp covered the entire roof and hung down on the sides a good couple of feet. Then we filled the space on three sides with the dirt piled up all around, using the shovels left there for us, and left open only the ramp to the entrance. Three Russian soldiers inside the hut were sleeping on straw, never even giving the slightest sign of interest in what was going on around them.

It was late in the afternoon when we dropped the cart off at the shed and returned to our tree on the little hill. We had not talked much during the entire procedure. Each of us had his own thoughts and I was busy with my bloody hands, trying to clean the cuts and bruises with my handkerchief and saliva.

Meanwhile, there were about twenty prisoners and eight Russian soldiers kept an eye on us. The rules were more relaxed. We could stand around in groups and talk. Some were smoking, some were talking with the Russians, laughing, trying to understand each other. I sat under my tree and chewed on a piece of bread without being hungry. Uncle Hans ate one of his sandwiches.

I had in my pocket the letter that had at its head the swastika and "Nationalsozialistische Deutsche Arbeiter Partei", the Nazi Party. Addressed to me and dated April 23, 1945, it was the request to appear at Party headquarters for a hearing. My refusal to help with the construction of tank traps to defend our city had caught up with me. I also carried with me the Russian translation of that letter. Such document, I thought, could be helpful to identify me as an anti-Nazi.

I reached for the letter in my breast pocket and slowly and nonchalantly I walked over to the Russian who seemed to be the officer in charge at this post. Everything was quiet and relaxed, the Russians seemed almost friendly. I took out the letter and showed it to the officer for him to read. He saw immediately the letterhead with the swastika and I went hot and cold at the same time. He was supposed to see the translation!

In a rage he turned on me. "Du Nazi!" He screamed further unintelligible curses and threats, shook his fist in my face, turned red with anger, stamped his feet and carried on like a mad man. Those around us, prisoners and soldiers alike, gathered and formed a circle to see what was going on. Onkel Hans remained at a safe distance.

Somehow I got the letter out of his furious hands and left him with only the hand-written translation. He wagged the paper in front of my face and kept up his tirade. Perhaps he can't read, I thought, and suddenly I had both sheets in my hand. It all happened so fast, I didn't quite know how.

Again I sat under my tree. The commotion over, everything quieted down. The whole uproar had only taken a few moments.

My uncle sat down next to me, the fear still showing in his face. "You've got to get rid of that letter," he said, "if it isn't too late already."

Would there be any consequences? I tore both papers in a thousand shreds and went behind one of the bushes on the side of the hill. I did as if I had to relieve myself, dug a hole with my foot in the soft soil and stuffed the bits of paper into it, then covered it up with dirt. Back under my tree, I hoped to have buried the entire affair.

Nothing further happened, but I felt insecure and unsafe and, yes, stupid for a long time afterwards

I destroyed what had seemed important to me, or of potential value. At a more appropriate occasion, if given at the right time into the right hands, the document might have provided me with some advantage. There was no reason to take the letter out of my pocket when I did; I had acted prematurely, stupidly, without thinking. There had been no interrogations, no frisking, no checking for ID's.

The weather continued gray and dismal. Evening was approaching. It may have been eight or nine o'clock when we suddenly heard them shouting, "Du, du, geh nach Haus! Alle geh nach Haus! Komm, schnell, schnell, nach Haus!"

All go home? Is that what they mean? We looked at each other, puzzled. What did this mean?

"Nach Haus! Schnell, schnell, alle nach Haus!"

What's going on here? The Russians roused us, herded us together in a group. Watch out, be alert, don't trust them. At last something was happening.

The waiting was over, but what did they have in mind? We were doubtful, suspicious. Four of the soldiers led us away from our tree, one of them on each side, one in front and one at the rear of our group. Darkness fell, the trees to our right formed a black wall.

"Something's wrong here," said Onkel Hans.

Someone else whispered, "We're close to the border, you think they'll really let us go?"

Another voice answered, "I don't believe it, we're still prisoners!"

Opinions went back and force. A young man had an idea. "Maybe we can run for it?"

"Psst, not so loud! Grab the chance, if you can."

"No, it's not dark enough."

The rain came down harder. We passed the shack where we had picked up the tarp earlier. A young couple came up to us and the man asked, "What do you think is going on? We are from Schwerin," he said. "We can't go back there. They would arrest us immediately!"

Onkel Hans shrugged his shoulders. He was about to answer something.

"Nicht sprechen!" A rough Russian voice cut him off, no longer friendly as a moment before. "No talking".

Now we knew. They had fooled us, just to quickly get us up and going. They grouped us closer together, holding the guns at their hips.

We entered the woods at the far end of the Palinger Heide on a narrow, muddy path just wide enough for horse and buggy, as the tracks showed. The forest became increasingly denser and it was quickly getting dark. On the winding trail we soon lost all orientation.

In a low voice I said to my uncle, "What are we going to do? I have no idea where we are. How can we get away? Damn, they've got us now!"

He was hopeless. "It's all over. We'll never see Rostock! They were right, nobody makes it alive!"

I didn't want to hear that. I wanted encouragement, a positive idea. Keep your eyes and ears open, I told myself, observe and be alert, let nothing escape you.

We marched on in silence, with only the sound of our steps in the mud, hitting a puddle now and then, or slipping over loose gravel, someone stumbling over an exposed root or a rock.

There was that steady rustle of the rain in the forest, that light, pleasant sound in the leaves above, then the heavier drumming of the larger drops hitting the ground.

A weak, flickering light appeared ahead, through the trees. As we came closer we discerned a kind of storm lantern on the porch of a house that could have been a hunting lodge in its better days. There were several soldiers. One of them sat under the lamp at a square table, with paper and pencil. Others were standing around, leaning against the railing, talking, smoking. A few steps led up to the porch. There were a lot of men, women and children, trying to get up the steps and out of the rain, but there wasn't enough room. A line led from the left to the table where the Russian soldier sat. My uncle and I had kept together all the time.

The soldier asked a few questions and took notes on the paper in front of him. Those who had been "processed" came down the steps on the right side, back into the rain. Steadily our group approached the steps to the porch. The Russians who had brought us here were watching, so no one could escape.

We advanced quickly. Soon we were on the steps, then at the table. The young Russian who sat there did not seem to be older than twenty; he looked friendly and intelligent. He spoke German.

"Name?"

"Haase, with two a's."

"First name?"

"Peter."

"Oh, that is Russian name!"

"Yes!" *Did I have a chance here? An advantage?*

"Where to?"

"Rostock." He wrote it all down.

"Next!" *No advantage then, after all.* I thought he had smiled when he said I had a Russian name. Behind me I heard: Godow, Hans. To Rostock.

Back in the rain, I noticed there were now only men. I looked around. Someone said, "Women and children are over there."

"Meine Frau! What's going on? What's happening here?" It was the young man from Schwerin. "I can't talk to her anymore? Where will we meet? Where are they taking her?"

We tried to calm him. Did they ever see each other again? Who knows? We were separated into smaller groups of ten or twelve, only men.

The night was completely black. We walked in single file and I could hardly see the back of the man ahead of me. The mud in the road was ankle deep. It rained without letting up and I was wet through and through. Four Russians, gun in hand, marched us along a narrow path through the dense forest. When we started out my uncle was behind me; I hoped he was still there.

The man in front of me stumbled over something. One of the guards pushed him back in line with his gun. I thought of the women and children. What will happen to them?

Nobody talked. Everyone seemed careful not to slide out of line. With every step I made sure not to leave my shoe behind in the mud. My footwear wasn't meant for this kind of outing.

I was wet and cold. *How much farther? For how long have we been walking already? How much longer did we have to go? One step after the other. When will it be morning? Will there be a morning?*

Something interrupted my thoughts. Something was happening. My senses were awake immediately. *What is this new situation? What can I do with it?* There were lights flickering to our left, coming towards us. We stopped. Some Russians came out of the woods, talking to our guards. They ordered us to empty our pockets and what we carried with us. I only saw the beams from their flashlights, the stuff that dropped into the mud and the searching paws. They shoved my knife aside. One of them frisked me.

As suddenly as they had appeared, they withdrew into the trees. Quickly I reached for my knife and stuffed everything back into my leather case, bread and socks, underwear and my shirt, all soaking wet and

51

muddy. Perhaps it was good that I no longer had the letter with the Swastika, I thought.

"Did they take anything?" My uncle asked me, whispering as I picked up my stuff.

"I don't think so. How about you?"

"I didn't do anything, just stood there. I don't think they even noticed me."

"The luck you have!" I said. He wasn't exactly the courageous type. "How do you get away with things like that?"

"I didn't want to throw my stuff in the mud. Nobody said anything, so I just stood there."

I could only shake my head. He was so naive. We were all quiet again as we continued our march, only here and there a grunt, a curse when someone stepped into a deeper puddle. Onkel Hans tipped me on the shoulder to show me he was still behind me. Two more times we were stopped, had to empty our pockets and bags under flashlights. The last time even Uncle Hans didn't get away so easily, but he had nothing that interested the grabbing paws. Only his last piece of bread got lost in the darkness, in the mud.

At last we came out of the forest and reached an asphalt highway. The rain had ended and, although it was still dark, I realized where we were. It had to be the farm Selmsdorf, across the road: main building on the left, farther back seemed to be the stables and to the right the big barn. In the middle, directly in front of us, a large, square yard, open to the road. The three-storied big house on the left gave the impression of former wealth, but the owners were long gone.

The very large barn was built in the style of the area, of red brick and wooden beams. The tall double door stood wide open towards the yard, an armed sentry in front of it. Just inside the door sat a Russian soldier at a table with an oil lamp on it and a writing pad and pencil. He seemed to have been waiting for us. Probably the same thing happens every night, I thought.

We had to put everything we carried with us on the table—he put my knife to the side. He wrote down our names, where from and where to. He did not say that I had a Russian name. After he finished with me I could collect all my stuff; I reached for the knife from behind his back.

A guard sent us into a side room already crowded with sleeping, snoring people. A thin layer of straw covered the floor. It was dark and we tried not to step on anybody.

"Quiet! Shut the door!"

"Shut up! Lie down and be quiet!"

"What's all that noise, waking us up here?"

Some continued snoring. Onkel Hans and I found a spot against a wall and we let ourselves down in the straw. My leather bag and hat served as a cushion for my head.

I was asleep instantly.

* * * * *

The morning was gray and depressing. The barn was crowded with prisoners. Where did they all come from? When had they arrived? There were over fifty men. I was probably the youngest among them. Still more arrived in the next hours. We were standing around in the vast open space of this huge barn, in groups, talking, guessing what would happen next. Russian soldiers were everywhere, in front of the barn, at the stables, in the big house across the yard, hanging out of every window. One Mongolian type with broad face and flat nose, strong as a bull, stood guard with his gun in front of the open door.

Some of us were ordered to do some chores. I had to sweep the concrete footpath and the stairs in front of the main house. While doing so I saw the barrier across the street, a roadblock with an armed sentry I had not noticed in the night when we arrived.

Then I was standing again at the open double door of the barn and listened to what people around me were talking about. Some were discussing the possibilities of getting away from here, a thought that had also occupied my mind ever since we had been caught in the Heide. Uncle Hans came back from the stables where he had to wash out milk cans. The sun made a weak attempt to come through the low hanging clouds. It was warmer than the day before and our damp clothes began to dry.

A truck drove into the yard and stopped in front of the barn. Some Russians in long, brown uniform coats sprang from the vehicle. Officers. They remained standing there and kept looking at us. Men from behind us pushed to the front, trying to get to the entrance to see what was going on. My uncle and I were in the first line, facing the yard.

"What are they looking at us for, like idiots?" someone said.

Another voice. "Something is going to happen, now that they are here."

Some of the soldiers fooled around on the yard with a bicycle. Like children tried to ride it, fell, laughed and tried again.

"They can't send us all to Siberia," said an older man, standing behind me.

The officers kept staring at us in the wide-open barn door.

53

"If they think we're trying to escape, they're right," Uncle Hans said to me.

"Let me try something here." I had an idea. "With my bag hanging from my shoulder I look like I'm ready to get out of here."

In a bored gesture and faking a yawn, I took the strap from my shoulder and let the bag drop carelessly to the floor. Then I leaned against the doorpost, giving the impression of total disinterest. I kept the Russians in the corner of my eye and saw how they turned around and walked towards the main building.

"Man, how that worked! What a trick!" Uncle Hans was perplexed.

"What did he do?" A man with an eye patch asked. He turned to me, "How did you do that?"

"A little trick of mine," I said, self-importantly, but I thought, it was probably just a coincidence. To Uncle Hans I said, "We have to get away, now or never."

He came up with the plan to step out to the right, behind the wing of the open door. "Then, close to the wall and out of sight into the bushes. Not more than five or six quick steps. In back of the barn we cross over to the highway."

I wanted to object, but he continued. "There are no more check points," he said. "Those who came from the other side said so. Just out of here, and we're free!"

I still had my doubts. "But how do we get away from here with that bull standing right in front of us?"

"That's only one second, than we're outside and behind the door, hidden from sight. Another second and you are in the bushes. We've got to try it!"

I was to go first. He would follow in two minutes. Then we would meet on the highway into the village. I picked up my leather bag and stepped around the door, keeping the bull from Mongolia in sight. He didn't move. I was afraid as I moved around the open wing of the door. At that moment the man with the eye patch said, "Maybe this would be the moment to get away."

As I sprang into the bushes I heard my uncle's voice, "My nephew's already gone."

I reached the shrubs but was still in full sight from the windows in the main house. I started to unbuckle my pants, squatted down and then, in two jumps, I was hidden in the bushes and hurried on. Behind the barn was an open meadow. I thought of the sentry at the roadblock and decided not to go across the field. Instead I made my way through some underbrush and came out at a sandy road. I was shocked to see a troop of about thirty Russian soldiers sitting and lying around in the dirt. Damned, I said under my breath, and turned around. Back to the meadow, my only choice. Again behind the barn, I crouched and started to cross the field, in open view of the sentry at the roadblock. I'm an easy target, I thought. Would he call out to me first? Or give a warning shot? *Don't think about it.* Stooping low, I ran towards the few trees bordering the highway. It wasn't far. Why didn't he shoot? Didn't he see me? The trees gave me some cover. I came to a wire fence—no problem, I had come this far. Easily I climbed over and came out on the asphalt road, some five hundred feet past the roadblock.

I was too exited to take in my new situation. Was I free? The anxiety had not left me. I did not feel secure yet. A farm girl pushing a bicycle came along and I asked her if I could walk with her.

"There's a soldier with a gun at the roadblock."

"They can't do you nothin' here," she said. "This side of the *Schlagbaum* ain't nothin' they can do!" She lived in Selmsdorf, she told me, and she knew her stuff. "You can walk along with me, if you want to."

I put my bag on her baggage rack, did as if we belonged together. "There's a bunch of Russians lying around in that side road coming up on the left", I said to her.

"Don't matter! They can't do nothin'! You can believe me!" She was beginning to get a little annoyed with me.

That's how I got into the hamlet of Selmsdorf.

*   *   *   *   *

It was late in the afternoon. People in this little, rural village were moving around free and unrestrained, pursuing their normal activities. The highway crossed another paved main country road. Small, neat houses lined both streets. There were a notion store, a grocery, a barbershop, a bakery, a machine repair shop, the tavern and a tobacco shop that also sold newspapers. I still had a strange feeling, walking around unrestricted, free and in the open. *But, where can I find Uncle Hans?* Did we perhaps miss each other when I did not immediately cross the field behind the barn to reach the highway? Or did they catch him as he tried to follow me?

I went into the bakery and asked the storeowner for a bread or some buns.

"Not without coupons," she said. Of course, how could I have forgotten. Ration stamps!

"And where can I get those?"

"Can't get any. Have to be registered here!" The bakery woman's information came slow and hesitantly.

"Well, where can I register? You see, I just got here—from over there,

55

you know."

"Must go to the *Bürgermeister*, along the street, across the main road, on the left side."

I thanked her. The village mayor lived in a little single house not unlike all the others. I knocked. A woman let me into a small, cozy living room. "He'll be right with you," she said.

I sat down at an oval table with a doily and dried flowers in vase on it. The furniture was old fashioned, or just old.

A farm worker in overalls came in. "Registration?" he asked. He was the *Bürgermeister*.

He wrote my name, date and place of birth on a form of soft, pink card board, and then entered: 5 August 1945, signed it and, most importantly, used a rubber stamp to place a seal in the lower left corner. The ink on his stamp pad was watery and hardly visible on the form. "Now you go and get yourself them traveler's coupons, at the office, down by the corner." He was smiling very friendly as he said that.

"Thank you, Herr Bürgermeister!"

I had become a resident of Selmsdorf. The house where the office was hardly looked different from all the other houses, except it was set at an angle at one of the four corners of the intersection. The door stood open. There was one large room where the residents could hold their meetings or go dancing on Saturday nights. Now, however, the whole floor was covered with straw, leaving open only a center lane. The hall was converted into a refugee camp. Just inside the door sat two young girls at a table, talking and giggling. This was the office. I showed my just-obtained residence card and, without questions, I got my traveler's ration coupons.

I went straight to the bakery: rolls, margarine, jam of some artificial flavor—all in the same store. I already felt like a human being again and began to have fun with my adventure. I could not buy milk at the dairy shop because I had no container, but I did get a glass of milk for a coupon. The woman didn't want any money.

A bunch of people came along the highway. I met them at the intersection. The one with the eye patch was among them. He told me, "Your uncle got out of there a minute after you left. He must have come through here a while ago."

How could we have missed each other? I should have seen him somewhere.

"There was no problem; we would have heard something," the man continued. "He must have kept on going without wasting time here."

He was probably right. "But how did you get here?" I wanted to know.

"Oh, that was easy. Shortly after you had sneaked out, they yelled, 'Alle geh nach Haus! Komm, komm!' Go home! All free to go! 'Schnell,

schnell!' and so two groups formed on the road and one went East, the other West."

"So, then there was no need for us to take that risk. They let everyone go, right?"

"Well, it wasn't quite that easy. You see, they had sent soldiers out ahead and after a hundred yards or so they chased us back in the opposite direction!"

"And now you're back where you came from? That's the trick they always use!"

"As the two groups met I could turn around, I was lucky. Maybe one or the other got away with it, but they were watching us pretty good!"

We parted and wished each other good luck. Smart fellow, I thought; but I would probably have gotten away with it, too. *What about Uncle Hans, though? Where could he be? Why didn't he wait here for me?* He must have thought I was the one who did not wait, since I was the first to leave.

Darkness fell late in the middle of summer. I guessed it was around ten o'clock when some street lamps came on, just glowing without shedding much light. From the windows in the houses also dim lights began to show. There were fewer people in the street; only in front of the tavern some men were standing around, arguing loudly. Noises of exited discussions came through the open windows, together with the smell of stale beer and cheap tobacco. I decided to stay overnight in the refugee hall, to set out early in the morning.

The straw filled hall was already pretty crowded, yet I found a place and, with my head towards the center lane, I lay down to reserve my spot. My leather case and my hat were my pillow. Only now I noticed how exhausted I was. After a while I got used to the hard floor. I became aware of a pain in my back and shoulders, which slowly subsided.

Before falling asleep, I reviewed in my mind the events that brought me to this place. When did all this start? Only yesterday morning? It seemed so much longer. What had happened? Palinger Heide. We were caught. We sat in the rain. The tarp and that underground hut. Then that scary incident with my letter. The march through the forest in the rain and the searching paws. The escape. The *Bürgermeister*. Where was Uncle Hans? *Haase with two a's.* I fell asleep.

When I awoke the lights in the hall were still on. *Or is it day already?* The door was open and outside was bright sunshine. I must have slept at least eight hours. I felt refreshed and wanted to get going right away. Maybe I had already lost valuable time, could have been underway for hours. I wanted to reach Rehna. I knew there was a railway station. Would I find Uncle Hans there?

I didn't think anybody would have a watch. I ate my last two rolls with margarine and jam, then stopped quickly at the dairy shop for a glass of milk. A clock on the wall showed a little after seven. I felt fine.

In the afternoon I came into the rural town of Rehna. I had walked along the highway for hours and hardly met a soul. No cars, only one or two horse drawn farm wagons. No Russians. *Uncle Hans must have come along this road yesterday*, I thought. *With luck, we will meet in Rostock.*

On the side of the road I had picked some berries. I had not eaten anything since early morning. The day was sunny and warm. Once I stopped at a water pump in front of a farmhouse, let the cool water run over my head. I took off my shoes and washed the hard, crusty mud from them. I felt blisters on my feet. I rinsed one foot after the other under the pump, without removing the socks. Refreshed, and with my shoes back on my cooled feet, I continued my long journey along the side of the asphalt road.

Rehna is a small country town. The highway cuts right through the middle. The side streets were paved with cobblestones and had clean sidewalks. The houses were small and well cared for. Not many people were outside. *It must be Sunday*, I thought, but wasn't sure. Children played behind white picket fences. It was a quiet little town.

I turned left, down a side street. After a few blocks I came to the railway tracks. On the right hand side was the train station. Four, five rail cars stood on a siding, as if they had been forgotten. Inside the small building, in the dingy waiting room, I found some two dozen people with cases, boxes, cartons, baskets and bundles—remnants of their possessions. Some of them had pushcarts or dollies loaded with the rest of what they had owned in their better days. Refugees. Perhaps they had spent weeks already in this neglected railway station, waiting for a train that might or might not come to take them some place else. They were mostly women, old women with black shawls around their heads and shoulders, and black, long dresses. There were some younger ones with small children and babies. Only two or three old men. Outside, in front of the station, which I had not seen before, since I had come over the tracks, there were more women watching their children as they played in the sun.

I approached the counter and behind the glass, much to my surprise, there was actually a clerk in blue railroad uniform with silver buttons. I had not expected that. *Who pays this man?* I wondered. *He's coming in to work as he has for half a century, even though there is no job.*

"Will there be a train?" I asked.

"Who knows," he said. "Sooner or later, maybe today, or tomorrow; perhaps next week."

Then I heard hissing and panting from outside; there was the clatter of wagons being coupled to a locomotive. *Could that be? Did I get here as if for a scheduled departure?* I was very exited. I had to be on that train, no matter what the destination or the time of departure. I knew it could only go east from here. I had some money sewn into the seam of my pants, under the belt. I ripped open the stitches to get to it.

"One ticket to Rostock," I said. "This train seems to be leaving. Where is it going?"

"There is no train going anywhere. Hasn't been one for over a week; besides, I have no tickets to sell," the man said.

"Then I'll get on without a ticket. I want to be on that train, just in case!" I ran across the platform, jumped over a couple of tracks and got into a car with the number '2' on it. That was once a second-class compartment, before the upholstered seats had been torn out. Now all that was left of them were the metal frames, and here and there a bent spring, a shred of fabric.

There were people in the car. They seemed to have lived here for some time, without being interested whether the train would go anywhere or kept standing where it stood. Most of them wore remnants of Wehrmacht uniforms.

I took my seat on a wooden plank that had been placed on the rusty frame and I leaned my head against my leather case at the window, which remarkably was still intact. I couldn't believe I had come this far. Scarcely an hour in Rehna, and I was on a train. That this train would actually move, however, I hardly expected.

Nonetheless, it did.

*   *   *   *   *

A few more people got on, but the train wasn't crowded. It wasn't long either—I had seen no more than half a dozen cars when I first arrived.

I felt nauseous, weak and a little dizzy. I had not eaten anything all day besides my rolls early in the morning, some berries and a green apple I had picked on the roadside to Rehna. I had no appetite, but I thought it might be better if I chewed on something. I scraped the mud of the Palinger Heide and the forest road from my bread, which had become rock hard. With my knife I broke little bits off and chewed them slowly. After a while I began to feel better.

I must have dozed off when a sharp, abrupt motion almost threw me off my seat. *Did this train just move?* Another jerk. I looked out the window and saw the stationhouse slowly slide past. Then there was an open field, some trees, a barn, more trees...

We were underway. Where to? Some of the people in the car said it would be Schwerin, others guessed Wismar. It did not matter to me; both towns were in the right direction. I felt certain I would make it to Rostock.

I dozed. Night had fallen. Sometimes a match flared up to light a cigarette or a pipe. Several times the train stopped on the open track, in the middle of nowhere. Then it moved again, often at not more than walking speed. I was tired, but I didn't want to sleep, with all those characters around.

After several hours we came into a larger station. It was Schwerin.

Hundreds of people crowded the platforms, shoving and pushing in every direction. The multitude moved down some stairs, through tunnels, up again to other platforms. A few dangling bulbs gave inadequate light in the steamy, polluted air. There were more trains, more people. I pushed my way through, like everyone else, not aiming anywhere in particular. People cursed and yelled, confused by wrong information, or no information at all. It was a terrible, disorderly mass of humanity. Locomotives hissed, belching smoke and steam.

In spite of all that noise, I heard it: Rostock. Where? Which train? Did I hear right? Several times now: Rostock. I asked. Nobody knew anything. But then, yes, this train was supposed to go to Rostock. Already overcrowded, people tried to get through the windows or they huddled on the running boards, others stood between cars on the couplings.

I had to get on this train—when would there be another? I was just pulling myself up on to the bumpers between two wagons when I heard it.

"Gert! Gert! Over here!" My name, only used in the family or among close friends? Here?

Couldn't be me; had to be someone else.

But then again, "Gert! Hurry! Here up front, there's room here!"

And then I saw him, hanging out from the open door of a freight car, wildly waving towards me with his free arm. Onkel Hans. Incredible! How could he have seen me in this tumultuous crowd, in the half dark? I forced myself through the throng. He pulled me up, other arms reached out, helping.

They made room for us in the middle, pushed boxes and suitcases together for us to sit on. I didn't understand this welcome, but slowly it became clear to me. These people had been in this rail car since noon and had already heard our story from Onkel Hans, at least his part of it.

"This is Gert, my nephew," he explained. "Something like this you can't even dream up, to meet here like this!" Well, yes, this was hard to believe.

They were all happy with us, eagerly listening as we recounted what happened. There were jokes and laughter, and questions, questions, questions.

The train started to move and was slowly pulling out of the station. I was telling my side of the ordeal, interrupting to answer their questions, and little by little our stories came together.

Then I turned to my uncle. "Now I want to know what happened to you."

He told us how he just walked out of the barn shortly after me and then, without hesitation, crossed the meadow.

"In full sight of the sentry at the roadblock?" I asked. "How is it that you didn't think he might shoot you?"

"Naw, that thought didn't even occur to me. Once I was out of that barn I felt completely safe!"

I thought, *how could anybody be so naive.* "But then you thought it would be too risky to stay overnight in Selmsdorf?"

"Yes, that's true, but I also guessed you must have gone right through without stopping, since there was no sign of you." He went on, "You had some nerve, to go to the *Bürgermeister* of Selmsdorf. Instead of giving you papers, he could have reported you."

"Well, right," I admitted and thought of that possibility for the first time.

And so this exiting exchange continued. Everybody was listening. A farmer had picked Uncle Hans up, took him on his wagon to Rehna and let him stay overnight at his house. In the morning he had breakfast with the family and then he was lucky enough to find a ride to Schwerin. By noon he already arrived at the train station.

When the train rolled into *Hauptbahnhof*, the main station of Rostock, it was still dark. There was a curfew until five o'clock. Russian soldiers and German auxiliary police did not allow arriving passengers out of the station. Onkel Hans and I spent a couple of hours in a broom closet, sitting on upturned buckets, dozing and reliving the events of the last three days.

At the first light of the new day we set foot on the pavement of our beloved town.

61

General-Litzmannastrasse (Hermannstrasse) 12

*   *   *   *   *

Like the three days in Hamburg, much of the three weeks I spent in Rostock is a blur in my memory. The morning I walked out of *Hauptbahnhof* onto the plaza in front of it, I felt lost. It dawned on me that I was a stranger in my own town.

Hans Godow immediately hurried to his home in Dierkow, a northeastern suburb, anxious to see his wife and his son. As the city was slowly coming to life on this early August morning, I found myself treading familiar pavement, yet everything seemed different. A red banner, announcing in oversized letters that **This City works in Solidarity and Friendship with the People of the Soviet Union** stretched across the façade of the *Hautbahnhof*. I walked the short distance to Hermannstrasse. Our nameplate had been removed from the mail slot. I read Goldschmidt where Haase used to be. Dejected, like an outcast, I turned away. Anyway, it was too early to ring somebody's bell.

Huge paintings of Stalin, Lenin and Molotov decorated official buildings, the *Rathaus,* the post office, police station and schools. Banners with slogans like **Peace and Progress under the Leadership of Worldwide Communism** adorned plazas and parks. Hammer and Sickle replaced the Swastika. The Soviet Star hung on city gates, landmarks and from hastily erected arches. Signs boasting of the achievements of the **Victorious Red Army** partially covered the scars of the air raids of 1942 and later bombings.

The Brunnemanns, our friends and landlords in Paulstrasse, had found humble dwellings in Doberanerstrasse. Herr Brunnemann's wholesale hardware business was destroyed in April of 1942 and he had retired. I directed my steps through the city and when I knocked at their door, Frau Brunnemann, aged into an old woman, had difficulty in understanding that I had come from "the West". I learned that Herr Brunnemann had died shortly after Rostock fell into the hands of the Soviets.

As I think back, it seems that I lived for three weeks in a state of semi-consciousness. I slept a few nights in a spare room at Frau Brunnemann's. Waking up on the third morning, I was covered with the itching bites of bedbugs. I fled, carefully examining my clothes for the pesky pest, and did not return to Doberanerstrasse. I looked up my girlfriend, Marianne. I had never been at her house before. Her mother, a nurse at a children's hospital, was usually on night duty. For several days she was unaware that I, a stranger, slept in her house and did not show much surprise when she found out. She seemed to be indifferent toward her daughter's activities and for the most part, she ignored me.

During the hot summer days of August, I divided my time between Rostock and Warnemünde. In retrospect, I find that I quite possibly spent more than one night sleeping on the beach. I discovered that Tatta's apartment was unoccupied, but I had no key.

I met my friend Hanning Löscher. "What? You are alive?" His face showed disbelief, even shock, and relief at the same time. "I was sure they had hanged you."

"What are you talking about?"

"You had disappeared. Your name was on the list. I saw it myself!"

"What list? There's a list?"

"You don't know? That list with names on the *Rathaus* door. Saboteurs and deserters, anti-Nazis. The last day the Nazis were in charge they hanged three men in public. Just before the Russians came in. Where were you?" He looked as if unsure it was me he was talking to.

"Remember I told you about that Wehrmacht transport? The day I came home from sailing they were waiting for me. My mother and I, we made it to Lübeck. I'm here illegally."

"Well, I am glad to see you." Then, hesitatingly, "So, Lübeck, huh? How is it there?" *Did I hear a little resentment, envy, even disapproval in his tone?* "I mean, it's pretty bad here."

"It's bad there, too. No food, no clothes, no phone, no electric or gas. Nothing. Political?" I whispered, "We're okay. What's going on here?"

"Ssht. Let's go. There are eyes and ears everywhere." We walked and dropped that subject.

Later I asked him, "What about Otto? Is he around?"

"Yeah, but I don't see him very often. He joined the Young Communists, something like that. Says, he wants to sail and he can't do that unless he joins. I rather not sail than join them."

I decided to legitimize my presence in the city by registering at the *Einwohnermeldeamt.* I gave   the address of Frau Brunnemann at Doberanerstrasse as my residence. Carefully I folded the document that identified me as a citizen of Rostock. Then, as a legitimate resident, I received my food ration stamps.

Some of the coupons I gave to Marianne, some to a friend of my father's whom I visited in his villa at Stephanplatz. Herr Gohlke, prominent Rostocker architect, was a much older man than my father. I found his imposing frame reduced to an emaciated shadow of himself. As a member of the former intelligentsia, he and his family were allowed only the lowest category of ration cards, not enough to keep a person alive without supplements of some kind.

"How did you come by this life-saving commodity?" He asked in his dignified manner of speaking, which seemed out of place under the circumstances.

"I registered as a resident at City Hall and then got my ration card. The normal procedure."

"What? You advanced into the lion's den? Nobody dares enter the halls of government."

"I thought nothing of it." I didn't know why Herr Gohlke was so taken aback by something that seemed absolutely ordinary to me. I learned gradually that most people avoided coming in contact with the new authorities, exactly the way non-conformists under the Nazi regime shied away from close encounters with those in charge.

Herr Gohlke produced a large suitcase. "Do me a favor, Gert." He addressed me by my first name only used in my family and by closest friends. "Take this back with you and see to it that my son in Hamburg gets it."

He obviously did not understand what a border crossing entails. "Herr Gohlke, I'm sorry, but that is quite impossible. I am not traveling by train, with a valid ticket, with a permit. There is no such thing as legally crossing the border. I have to hide, crouch and run. By night. The *Grüne Grenze* is risky business. I can't carry that suitcase. Please, understand."

Clearly, Herr Gohlke had lost his grip on reality. His once brilliant mind had shriveled as had his body. He mumbled something like, "I must tell your father of your refusal; he will have a word with you."

"I am sorry, Herr Gohlke," I said as he turned his back on me.

Yachtclub, with view of Rostock across the Warnow

I went back to Hermannstrasse. For a long time I paused in the vacant lot, where a villa had stood before a single bomb had reduced it to rubble. I looked at the house that had been our home for the last three years. There were different curtains at the windows of the first floor. I walked across the street and rang the bell next to the name Goldschmidt. I entered and climbed the stairs. In the open door stood a young, petite woman.

"Frau Goldschmidt, I am Peter Haase. I used to live here with my family. May I come in?"

What an awkward feeling, my apartment, and I have to ask permission to come in?

She stepped aside, surprised but in full control of herself. "Come in. What is the purpose of your visit?" For a small, pretty person she had an unexpected strong voice, perhaps grown harsh in a concentration camp.

"Thank you. I did not come to claim any of our things. I just wanted to see our apartment one more time. We left in such a hurry, you know."

"Your apartment? It is my apartment. I have the right to be here, not you. Since you left it, the housing commission assigned to me." In spite of the hard words and her strong voice, she did not seem aggressive, only clear and assertive. She let me walk through the rooms. I touched a chair, a crystal vase, the couch on which I had lain in my plaster mold. Most of it was the way I had last seen it a little over three months ago.

In the kitchen I remarked, "Our red tea kettle..."

"My tea kettle," Frau Goldschmidt corrected me.

"I am sorry," I said.

She opened a wardrobe. "Is this your mother's?" She pulled out a black dress elaborately adorned with lace and embroidery. "You may have it. Perhaps it means something to your mother."

"My mother's cocktail dress." She had worn it at Dieter's and my confirmation and once to a party she attended with my father at the officer's club. "She will be happy and thankful to you."

"Well, take it." She wrapped it in paper and handed it to me.

I left Frau Goldschmidt's apartment and went upstairs. In the attic, where I had my bedroom, there was a small apartment. Frau Levetzow lived there with her teenage son. I knocked.

"Oh, Herr Haase—sind Sie es? Is it really you?"

"It's me, all right," I said. I never liked that woman, always snickering around, gossiping and watching through the crack of a slyly opened door, or from behind a curtain. "How are you?"

"Oh, not good at all. It is terrible with the shortages and all. Have you come back? You know, you no longer have your place downstairs. They gave it to that Jew. I wish you could come back."

Hypocrite. She knew we were never friends. "I see you have saved that tablecloth for us. It's my mother's favorite! How nice. How about silverware?" I quickly opened a drawer of the kitchen cabinet, then another. "Oh, thank you, that was nice of you." I grabbed forks and knives with my father's initials. "I would like to take all you have saved for us, but unfortunately I can't carry it. I have to go back across the border, you know." I was right, this thieving bitch had taken advantage of our absence. *How much more has she stolen? And she's getting away with it.*

Frau Levetzow's jaw dropped, but she caught herself. "I thought you would come back for it."

As I was leaving, I spotted in a corner a pair of knee-high boots, which I recognized as my brother's. "Oh, but I can take those. That's great, these shoes of mine have just about had it. Through the mud, in the rain, and then walking for endless kilometers. I'll wear these on my trip back."

The landlord, Herr Göldenitz and his wife lived on the ground floor. I passed their door without knocking. My mission at number twelve Hermannstrasse was done. A bundle with my mother's dress, a tablecloth and silverware under my arm and my brother's boots in hand, I left and walked away without looking back.

My time in Rostock had come to an end. "Three weeks," I had promised, "and I'll be back."

PART THREE
What now?

Neither Kurt nor I had permits to set foot in this area so close to the border. The ten to fifteen-kilometers-wide corridor, the no-man's-land, ran along the eastern side of the line separating the Russian and the British zones. This border later became known as the Iron Curtain.

Kurt had come from Russia. He either escaped or was released from a prisoner of war camp. He wasn't sure how long he had been on the road already. I met him as I was about to board a train in Schwerin. He stood on the bumpers between two cars and reached out to help me as I tried to climb up. The train was so crowded, people were hanging out the windows, standing on the running boards and on the couplings. Kurt, I noticed, was a little slow, or dull, but good-natured. In his early twenties, he may have been three or five years older than I.

We jumped off when the train stopped on the open track, rushed across a field and came to a rural highway. An endless column of Russian troops moved westward with trucks, cars, motorbikes and guns. In August of 1945, the border was still flexible. Nobody knew where it would be from one day to the other. Walking alongside the Russian troops, like two farmhands looking for work in the next village, we overtook them as they halted frequently. I carried my old leather bag with the treasures retrieved at Hermannstrasse and wore my brother's boots. Kurt had a dirty, once white blanket hanging over his shoulder, the ends tied together.

Overnight we stayed in a ramshackle hut at a refugee camp. There were only women and children and they lived in sad conditions. Without money or food, they existed on what they could find or steal in the fields: Cabbage, potatoes, turnips. I offered some money, but they would not take it unless they could give something in return.

"You have any tobacco?" I asked one of the young women.

"Yes, we can get some." She sent out a couple of kids who came back with an armful of green leaves.

"Tobacco! Just dry it in the oven for a few minutes."

Kurt crumbled a toasted leaf and stuffed the crumbs into his little black pipe. I rolled mine in a strip of newspaper, the way the Russians do. It was an acrid smoke.

On the back of his shaven head Kurt had a tremendous, poorly healed scar that showed under the re-growing hair. One of his feet was a bloody mess.

In the morning, over breakfast of roasted turnips, he took off his boot. I couldn't tell what was skin, flesh or sock, covered with mud and remnants of boot leather. He never complained.

That afternoon we came into a small village and hid in a barn. A farmwoman gave us some bread and ham and a mug of cow-warm milk. Later we went out on a spy mission to find out how close we were to the border. Some of the troops we had met the day before were also in the village and a Russian lieutenant stopped us. He spoke German.

"I saw you yesterday ten kilometers back on the road. I remember the blanket." He nodded towards Kurt. "You trying to cross border!" He was friendly, not threatening, but intimidating just the same.

"No," I protested. "We are looking for work." Kurt was dumbfounded, but said nothing. The Russian turned away and paid no further attention to us.

I said to Kurt, "That blanket has to go. See if we can get something for it."

He didn't care. He was glad to have found someone to take charge. We still had a few hours before darkness and went from house to house offering the blanket for something to eat. The woman at the third house down the road gave us a dozen eggs and some good pieces of bacon for the blanket.

"How far is the border and how can we best reach it?" I asked her. "Do you know?"

"They moved it last night two kilometers from here," she said. "See that great tree at the end of my garden? That's where you turn left. It takes you less than twenty minutes to the next farm. Before you see the houses you're in the English zone."

We thanked her and left her house through the back door. It was starting to get dark. In the mild night we sat under the big tree, sucking raw eggs, waiting for total darkness. We watched a small group of people in the distance, silhouetted against the night sky. They walked briskly in the direction we were to take and we followed them after a while, but saw no more of them.

There was a light drizzle and it was pitch black. We walked at a normal pace on firm, sandy ground. There was no road. A few times we had to lie down flat on the ground as a searchlight swept across the ghostly landscape. We saw the beam easily in the misty air. *The lieutenant—looking for us?* We went on until we saw the dark shapes of houses directly in front of us, dim lights behind curtained windows.

That was easy! Less than half an hour and without a problem. We walked to the main building, up a few steps, and knocked at the door. There was no response. I knocked again. Nothing. To the left were some smaller houses. In one of them a window stood half open. No light inside. *Perhaps we can spend the night here.* I reached in to unhook a lever.

A voice in German from inside, "Hey, what's going on? Who's there?"

Startled I said, "Sorry. I thought nobody was here! We need shelter for the night. Just came over from the Russian zone. Can we come in?"

The voice came back: "You're still in the Russian zone! They just set up a temporary *Kommandantur* in the big house."

That scared the hell out of me. "Holy shit!" I uttered under my breath. "We just banged at the door of the Russian command post? They didn't open the door."

Kurt showed little reaction.

"You better get going," the man continued. "Down along here, then right. You come to the highway. On the left you can see a roadblock, the English border post."

We never saw the man who spoke. "Thanks," I whispered. We hastened down the path along a couple more houses, farm workers' dwellings.

That was close! Kurt kept up with me and he was quiet, the way I wanted it.

We came to the corner, turned right, carefully looking in both directions. After a few paces we saw a strange, black shadow a foot wide, across the road. I stooped on my hands and knees and found a perfectly straight ditch, the wet, dugout dirt neatly piled up behind it.

Tricky bastards! I could make it in one jump, but Kurt had to make it, too. I made sure he understood.

"There might be a wire behind it." I spoke in a hushed voice. "I'll go first. Wait for my signal. And quiet!"

I jumped easily over ditch and sand pile, then kneeled. There it was, just below knee height. With my outstretched hand I felt a thin wire. I motioned for Kurt to jump and stop next to me. I held on to him as he landed a little unsteadily on his injured foot.

Lifting my foot high to clear the wire, I gestured for him to do the same. We listened. Everything remained still. There was only the light rain, and my heart throbbing in my throat.

The obstacle behind us, we continued on the sandy path, tall hedges on both sides. After some hundred meters we reached the highway, a paved country road. Before leaving the protection of the hedge we heard to our right a cough and spitting, then heavy boots on the asphalt, walking away. We waited, peeked out and saw nothing.

We turned left along the shoulder of the road. A flickering red lantern in the distance looked at first like the Soviet Star. We approached carefully. I was uncertain until I saw two soldiers wearing British military overcoats. Smoking and talking, with their backs to us, they were leaning against the white and red painted bar across the highway.

"Leave it to me, don't say a word. I have to figure this out as we go along," I whispered to Kurt. I had no idea what would happen. This was a critical moment: Will they let us pass, send us back or hand us over to the Russians? What are their orders regarding civilians that show up at their post?

I cleared my throat: "Hello!"

They turned around, very much surprised. "Hello! Where do you come from?"

I said, "From Mölln."

"No," one of them answered. "Mölln is over there, but you come from there." He indicated opposite directions with his outstretched arms.

Oh shit, I thought. "We got lost. Where are we?"

They exchanged glances. The first one said: "You come from the Russian zone. In fact, you're still standing on Russian soil!"

I acted horrified, bent down and came up on their side of the barrier, dragging Kurt with me.

"I am in search of my parents. They were supposed to be in Mölln, but they weren't." A believable story. At the end of the war so many families where separated, ripped apart and wandering all over the country, trying to find each other. "This is Kurt; we just met in Mölln."

I could see, they didn't know what to do with us.

"We're on our way to Lübeck," I continued. "Got lost in this messy, rainy night." I don't think they believed a word I was saying, but I lied so fluently in my school English, I almost convinced myself. Kurt looked baffled; he had no idea what was going on.

The two soldiers were debating. Then one of them told us, "You can sit in the sentry box, if you like."

With our legs sticking out in the light but steady rain, we sat in the little white and red striped box when a woman and her daughter showed up.

"Come, you can interpret." One of the soldiers called me over.

It was unfortunate for the women not to lie. They pleaded. They were begging, with tears in their eyes.

Should I lie for them? But how could I? What story could I make up on the spot to fit those dramatics?

One of the soldiers gave us a canvas tarp and took Kurt and me to a little shack down the road. "Better for you here, out of the rain," he said. "Bring the tarp back in the morning and don't go on before daylight. The Polish troops farther down that way shoot at anything that moves in the dark!"

We covered ourselves with the tarp. Kurt slept, but I was too excited. As it became lighter we took the canvas back to the border post. The two women were still there. Kurt gave the soldiers the slab of bacon the farmer's woman had given him. They were moved by his gesture, and so was I.

The rain had stopped. We started out on the highway to Lübeck, sadly leaving mother and daughter behind.

Walking most of the day, getting a ride only a couple of times for short distances, it was late afternoon when we arrived in Lübeck. Kurt and I said good-bye. He had a long way to go to Neumünster where his father had a small farm. Grateful for having helped him through no-man's-land and to freedom, he gave me his little black pipe.

I went home. My mother opened the door. She looked at me as if I were a ghost. She had all but given up hope to ever see me again.

I often think of Kurt. For many years I cherished his little black pipe.

* * * * *

During my absence of three weeks my father had returned from Norway. The British were bringing all German troops back to Germany and held them temporarily in camps, called Reservations. My father was in such a reservation in the woods near Lübeck.

There were no buildings or huts, only a primitive latrine. The prisoners-of-war began cutting down branches and twigs from the trees and built the most rudimentary shelters. A simple wire fence separated the men from the outside world while the process of releasing them took place in quick succession. The camp had to be vacated in a timely manner in order to accommodate new arrivals.

From the preconceived plan my father knew where to find us. The news that I had returned to Rostock, deep in the Russian occupied zone, devastated him. His words were later related to me. "Dieter was captured and he goes voluntarily... Now we lost them both."

My reception was accordingly both somber and happy. My father, roused from his nap—my parents had been in the woods that morning to gather firewood—looked at me in disbelief. Only slowly did he seem to realize that I was not an apparition or a dream.

Tante Irma came into the living room. Her reaction was spontaneous. "Gert, thank God, you are safely back." She called me by my familiar name and hugged me tightly.

"I knew he would make it," said Tatta as a tear rolled down her cheek.

"Here, I brought you this." I pulled a slab of bacon from the bundle I carried. "And look, your cocktail dress, Mutti! There's more, remember this tablecloth? Vater, the silverware. I found it at Frau Levetzow's, that thief. Dieter's boots, too. I wore them all the way back."

Then I answered all their questions. There were so many, it actually took days to tell them all that had happened: my wild experience on the way over, my arrival in Rostock and what I found there, and then the return. Frau Brunnemann, Frau Goldschmidt, Frau Levetzow, my friend Hanning Löscher, Herr Gohlke. (I mentioned Marianne only fleetingly.)

"I saw Onkel Hans briefly before I left Rostock. They are all right."

I told them about Kurt. "He will be home tomorrow, maybe tonight. His parents will be happy."

My talk of Kurt brought silence to the room. *Was it insensitive of me to mention Kurt?* There was no news about Dieter.

My father was disillusioned and embittered over the senseless war and the devastation it had caused in the world, to our nation and our lives.

The outlook was grim. The ancient family business was no more. His military career had ended abruptly. Without a home of our own, my father faced the future with uncertainty and often carried the burden in silence.

Schools opened, but I was reluctant to enroll for classes in the *Johanneum* and tried my hand at dentistry, assisting a neighborhood dentist in his laboratory repairing broken dentures. It could have become a career for me, if the guild had admitted new dental lab trainees.

I took up again my activities on the black market and became involved in the trade of MOC, a laundry powder. Carrying two large suitcases, I conveyed the contraband commodity from the railway depot to a distributor. For transportation I used the city buses and once a *razzia*, a police raid, was in progress at one of the bridges, but the bus I was riding was not inspected.

My father came home with an old sheepskin lining of an army greatcoat. "Clear the table," he said. "I am going to convert this thing into a lady's coat."

"No tools, no sewing machine? How?" asked my mother, but my father, the furrier with a military mind, was able to improvise even under the most primitive circumstances.

"I met a Polish woman on the street. She carried this fur over her arm. I asked, 'What do you want to do with that?' And she said, 'I want to wear it in the winter.' So, I thought, I can make something out of it."

"How?" my mother repeated.

"I have a pocket knife, Irma has needle and thread. That's all I need." With that he started to take the shaggy old coat lining apart.

Days later I brought the lady's fur coat to an apartment near the old barracks and returned with a sack full of canned goods, flour, sugar, real coffee and a pound of Danish butter. It was the beginning of my father's new enterprise.

In the fall I joined the classes already in progress at the *Johanneum*. At eighteen, my scholastic abilities had not improved from my earlier years and I was barely hanging on. One day a recruiter from the Lübeck Opera house came to the school, asking for volunteers to participate in a production of the opera Carmen. I, always looking for diversions, was among those who raised their hands. My career as an extra lasted through twenty-five Carmen performances and a season of Tannhäuser and Die Meistersinger as well as several plays.

Besides the interesting activities on- and off-stage, a most vibrant black market existed behind the wings. From ration coupons to clothing and shoes, from bicycles to fake ID's and of course cigarettes—everything was available. I had a source for syrup and jams and conducted a brisk business at the theater, in school and from home.

I do not recall how my father got in touch with Ferdinand Kurth, the former commander of the fortress of Rostock who had surrendered the city without bloodshed.

"You go to Hamburg," he told me, unwilling in his depression to return to the recent past.

Limited rail service re-established, I went to Hamburg by train and found Herr Kurth employed at the Olsdorfer *Friedhof*, the cemetery famous for the beautiful park-like landscaping. Colonel Ferdinand Kurth, severely wounded in battle, was now a gravedigger. I remembered him in his immaculate uniform, always wearing a smile in spite of constant pain. The smile and his elegance were still evident, even in gravedigger's baggy clothes.

We sat down for a while in a shack. He told me about his harrowing ordeal of escape from both the Nazis and the Russians and how he, hidden under hay in barns by day and tracing his way through the frontline by night, ended up in Hamburg's suburb, Olsdorf.

The news of refugee repatriation was at first a vague rumor, but then the talk of a rail transport into the Russian occupation zone became widespread. Tatta was determined to return to her home and we knew how unhappy she was, ripped from her home in Warnemünde. She had endured over a year in Lübeck and no one understood her homesickness better than I.

We obtained the necessary forms for her at the repatriation office and Tatta applied for the first transport.

I believe it was in the spring of 1947—the weather was already unseasonably warm—that my mother and father brought Tatta to the station. With one small suitcase and a bundle containing a blanket and a pillow, she embarked on the journey back home.

"How will she survive? Those were freight cars, for God's sake." My father was outraged. "And she's eighty-three years old."

"There were benches and they all had their blankets and cushions." My mother tried to convince herself that Tatta would be all right.

A month after she left we received a postcard from her. She had arrived in Warnemünde. From other sources we found out that the train had taken a week to reach Rostock and that the conditions had been indescribable. I had seen a refugee train a few months before the end of the war. I knew what it must have been like for Tatta.

Last visit with Tatta in Warnemunde (1954)

Last visit with Tatta in Warnemunde (1954)

∗   ∗   ∗   ∗   ∗

Twice in 1947, I undertook the increasingly difficult and dangerous nightly border crossing into the eastern part of Germany. Through my black market activities I had become acquainted with a gang of smugglers who transported black market products into the Russian Zone and returned with vodka, gin and other alcoholic beverages, still under prohibition in the West. I joined them, spent several days in Rostock and returned both times without incident. Evidently, the smugglers had some understanding with the VoPos, the East German border police.

In the summer of 1948, when the sudden, but anticipated, economic reform occurred, I was once again on a visit to Rostock. I had information that the VoPos in charge of a stretch of beach along the border, turned a blind eye and let people pass in both directions. However, that hole in the Iron Curtain was plugged by the time I tried to slip through.

A VoPo stopped me at midnight on the beach. "Sorry, but I've got to take you in."

"What happened? You won't let me pass? I heard..."

"The Russians were here two nights ago. They caught over fifty people. They're checking us out now. Come on, let's go. If I don't bring you in, it's Siberia for me." He marched me off to a waiting truck where I shared the fate of twenty others. By dawn, there were about three dozen men, women and children on that truck.

In the morning we arrived at a border control post, a farmhouse. Russian troops and German police swarmed about the place, guarding well over one hundred prisoners, crammed into a loft. The windows were boarded, and they locked the single door. A feeble light came from a bulb hanging under the ceiling. The room was so crowded that, when one of the men had an epileptic seizure, there was no room for him to lie down on the floor. Standing, and supported by those closest to him, he foamed at the mouth and soiled his pants.

The ordeal lasted into mid-afternoon. VoPos started to release us, ten at a time. Those, who presented documents identifying them as West German residents, were sent back to a checkpoint. I showed the already brittle paper I had obtained in Rostock on my first visit three years earlier. Among those with East German papers, I walked to the railway station, accompanied by a German VoPo. A train, consisting of no more than three or four wagons, was ready to leave. Before I could board, a very polite Soviet officer, elegant in his impeccable uniform, examined my paper, folded it carefully and handed it back to me. With a smile in his Mongolian face, he said in broken German, "Please, you enter train now."

Tatta received me in her home in Warnemünde. Eighty-four years old,

78

she began to lose some of her mental faculties, occasionally confused me with someone else and had no longer a sharp understanding of what was going on in the world. She ate little, shrunk to a tiny person of no more than eighty pounds and had difficulty leaving her second floor apartment to buy her groceries. Yet, her spirit was good and she showed no sign of physical ailments. She remembered things of the past, could still recite poems in the old regional language and talked of her America voyage nearly ten years ago.

Marianne was engaged to a man I had met once the year before. Walli Waldenburg, a bus driver, was often absent for days or a week and when that happened, I stayed at Marianne's.

The last night before my return to Lübeck I spent with Marianne. In the morning she accompanied me to *Hauptbahnhof.* I had missed the early local train to Schwerin, the one for "ordinary" people. The next train was an *Eilzug,* for which a permit was necessary to obtain a ticket.

"I have to be on that train," I said to Marianne.

"You can't do that. No permit, no ticket? You'll get arrested."

I wanted to show her how daring I could be. "I'll get on that train, watch me." With that I gave her one last hug and disappeared in the crowd moving through the ticket control and onto the platform.

The train was crowded. People in business suits, with briefcases. All seats were taken. I stood near a window among important looking travelers, maybe on official state or party assignment.

"Train's so crowded again. I am sure there are people without permits," said one.

"Yeah, remind me to make a report. The controls are too lax," another answered.

Surely, they are talking about me. In my drab outfit... Do I look like I belong on this train?

A conductor scrambled along on the running board of the slow-moving train. He passed by the window and opened the door to the next compartment. "Tickets," I heard him call out.

How lucky can you get! I thought of Marianne and wished she could have been there.

It was my last visit to Rostock and never I saw Marianne again.

In Schwerin I boarded another train. I felt confident. *What ticket? I don't need a ticket.* Luck was on my side.

In the early evening the train stopped at a rural station. Schönberg read a sign. The border was close and it was the end of the line. All passengers had to get off. VoPos were on the platform and inside the terminal. There were police also on the other side. I saw no escape. With the flow of the crowd I reached the VoPo checking for IDs. I pulled out my tattered Rostock residence paper.

"What's this?" He looked as if he had never seen such paper before. "Where's your ID?"

"That's it. There is no other ID."

"They issued ID cards long ago."

"Not in Rostock," I said and didn't know where my audacity came from.

"So, what are you doing here?"

"I have to see Doctor Schultz." *What am I saying? Where does this stuff come from? What if he asks...*

"All right. Go ahead." He handed me my paper and I walked as if in slow motion, on air rather than on firm ground, toward the exit. *Is this for real? Who is Doctor Schultz?*

Leaving the station and the few houses behind, I met a man going my way, crossing the railroad tracks. "Going to Hamburg?" he asked me.

"Lübeck," I said.

"I have done this many times. Come along."

Walking on the tracks was very uncomfortable. The ties were too close for a normal step, but too apart to skip one. A kilometer or two out of Schönberg, in the gathering darkness, there was a call from the right, out of the shadows. "Halt! Bleiben Sie mal stehen!" Stop right there!

The man from Hamburg bolted from the track down the embankment. I followed him. He found an opening through a tall hedge and kept running. I was stuck in the gnarled, stiff branches and by the time I had disentangled myself, my guide was nowhere to be found. A rifle shot rang in the still air. A sudden sharp pain in my left knee stopped me from running.

Examining my pant's leg for a hole or blood, I found nothing, but the pain continued and I could not bend my knee. I wasn't shot, so why this pain?

I listened. There was no sound of anyone following me. My companion was gone and whoever fired the shot did not come after me. I was sure that the path along the hedge would lead me back to the track, but walking had become very difficult and painful. I limped along and felt my left leg swelling from the thigh down to the ankle.

A light came from behind me. Still at a distance, I was aware it had to be a patrol, perhaps alerted by the single gunshot. In an adventure novel I once read that someone had made himself inconspicuous by blending into a bush. Assuming a crooked position, like the gnarled branches of the hedge, I pressed myself into the shrubs. I heard the wheels and the straining chain of a bicycle. "...And close your eyes, lest they reflect the light," I remembered from the story. The bicycle rider passed me at arm's length. Looking after him, I saw a rifle slung on his back.

Slowed down considerably by my painful, swollen left leg, I had to hurry to make it across the border before daylight. I found the railroad tracks again and continued westward. At the last station before the border, I crouched through the gardens between some houses and then reached the highway. I waited behind a bush as two Russian sentries walked loudly along the asphalt toward the checkpoint, and then I limped across. Only the ditch, formerly denoting the border between Mecklenburg and Schleswig-Holstein, now the frontier between East and West, separated me from the British zone.

The water was high in the ditch. With great difficulty and in pain I removed my pants, climbed down into the cold and murky water and up on the other side as dawn was creeping over the landscape.

It was August the nineteenth, my father's birthday. It was also the first day of school after the summer vacation. Before going to school, I went to see a doctor.

"Looks like you got stung by two hornets. One of the stingers is still in there, you see?" He put some dark brown, tar-like ointment on my knee and bandaged it. "That stinger will come out eventually."

The stinger did come out—years later.

My mother with Tatta in Warnemunde (ca 1948)

Sailing around Denmark, 1950
Jugen drinking,
Myself facing camera, partially hidden by bottle

* * * * *

During my absence the new Deutschmark had replaced the Reichsmark.

My father was able to build a new type of business, combining manufacturing and wholesale of semi-finished fur products.

I visited the Kurths once more in Hamburg. They had moved into a small garden apartment near the cemetery, where he had become the manager. Frau Kurth wrote and illustrated children's books.

I told them of my decision to leave school, enter the fur trade in Frankfurt and eventually join my father's business.

Herr Kurth tried to convince me to stay in school. "Is it the money?" he asked. "We would be able to help you."

I thanked them. "I am not very good in school and not at all sure that I would pass the Abitur. It would be a waste, especially now that they added a ninth year to make up for time lost during the war."

What a nice gesture it was, but my father found himself unwilling, or unable, to nurture this friendship. Why? Was the past too painful for him? Did he want to distance himself from everything that happened then? The loss of business and home, his military career? The uncertainty about Dieter?

In August of 1950 I moved to Frankfurt, but not before sailing around the Danish islands. My childhood friend, Jürgen Zander, now attending university in Kiel, asked me to join him and a group of students in a ten-day cruise on the Baltic Sea.

Herr Sprengel, of chocolate and candy fame, owned the INDIA. He granted the use of his thirty-six foot yacht to the members of his old fraternity Holsatia at the University of Kiel. This cruise was my first experience in ocean sailing; an experience I could not pass up even though it could cost me my job at a fur trading company. My employer, however, found my decision to postpone the start of my employment over a sailing adventure "impressive and refreshing".

I began my three-year stint in the center of the European fur business, Frankfurt. Hans Pinkert received me with a smile and a handshake that almost broke my wrist. He was strong and powerfully built, with blue eyes and slightly graying blond hair. His attitude toward me and my delayed arrival and the informal way in which he talked and listened to me put me at ease.

In his office space, which he shared with other fur companies, bundles of furs hung from the ceiling and stacks were piled on the floor. A wide table stretched under the window front of this third-floor, warehouse-like loft. With a minmum of instructions he put me to work. My first assignment was sorting gray foxes by color, character and fullness of hair. I had never done such work and was surprised to find that distinguishing the fine differences in nuances and structure of the furs was natural to me. Both my grandfathers had been furriers and fur merchants. I came from a long line of ancestors in this trade.

Hans Pinker was full of energy and I learned soon that he also had a temper to be careful of. He was unpredictable and sometimes disappeared for days. His secretary, the only employee besides me, did not know his whereabouts and neither did customers, suppliers or friends.

During one of his absences I moved the office to a new location, which Herr Pinkert had rented but did not occupy for two or three months. Our space had become so crammed with furs that it became difficult for me to do any work. I took the initiative and transferred the business to the new premises.

On his return—I believe he had been in London—he accused me of making decisions without his approval. "Why don't you put your nameplate on the door? You seem to be taking over." Expressions of anger and amusement alternated in his face.

84

My parents in Frankfurt, 1953

I had expected him to appreciate my action and, although he did in a way, our relatuionship cooled considerably.

One day I heard the name Krischer being mentioned as I visited a firm I did business with. "Frau Willert," I asked the office manager, "did you say, that's Herr Krischer talking to your boss? Benno Krischer?"

She said, "Yes. Do you know him?"

"I think so," I answered and walked over to the group of men talking. "Excuse me, Herr Krischer, my name is Peter Haase, the son of Richard Haase from Rostock."

He knew immediately who I was. I revealed to him that my father was trying to build a new business in Lübeck, and he told me briefly of his escape from Germany in November of 1938. He reached the USA via England, Pakistan and India, and now had a business in New York.

"I want to leave Germany," I told him. "I don't think there is much of a future for me here."

He introduced me to Mr. Rosen, an associate of his. "You want to work for him in London?" Mr. Rosen said, it could be arranged.

It turned out that British labor law allowed me to work in England under the condition that the money for my living expenses would come from Germany. My father could not guarantee a fixed monthly payment and so that possibility fell through.

Herr Krischer was eventually instrumental in facilitating my resettling in New York—but that,was many years later.

During my years in Frankfurt I lived in great poverty. As a volunteer apprentice, I received at first a minimal wage. My father, struggling to stay afloat in the new business world, had to supplement my meager income, but too often the money came hesitatingly, late, or not at all. I collected bottles, worked nights at a furrier's, bought discarded fur remnants with borrowed money and resold them.

A year and a half I worked for Hans Pinkert and learned much about furs and the business. Eventually I quit my apprentice job for a slightly more lucrative employment with the result that my father sent even less money.

I returned to Lübeck and joined my father's stagnant business. Enthusiastic, full of fresh ideas and with innovative approaches, I entered an atmosphere of gloom and doom. My parents had received the unofficial notice of my brother's death in Russia. Apparently overcome by pneumonia, with inadequate nutrition and medical care, he had died in January of 1947.

What little success my father had achieved in his new venture fell apart. The German *Wirtschaftswunder*, the economic miracle, passed us by. He was no longer capable of keeping in step with the competition,

86

unwilling to take risks, to accept new ideas. One by one, we had to let the twelve employees of our firm go.

A broken man, my father did some repair work and alterations. My life was at a dead end. One day, in one more attempt to drum up new business, I returned from Hamburg with a reasonably promising proposal to represent a fur wholesaler.

"Too risky. We have to invest money. That involves a bank loan. I won't do it."

"What about me, then? I have to make a living somehow." The Hamburg firm would not give me the representation without my father's involvement. "I am twenty-seven years old and I have no future."

He took a letter from his breast pocket. "Why don't you read this first? It came in the mail today."

The letter my father handed to me was from a distant relative in Ecuador.

I had met this man, Otto Schwarz, years ago in Frankfurt when he was in Germany on a business trip. Back in Lübeck, with no prospect of keeping our business afloat, I wrote to him, "Is there perhaps a possibility for me to come to Ecuador?"

As I sat in my father's office telling him about my meeting in Hamburg, I unfolded the letter.

My eyes flew over the half page, two paragraphs. The sentences were short, clear and left no questions. "Get in touch with so-and-so in Hamburg. He will give you two hundred marks to buy some tropical outfits. Your passage is booked. The banana freighter PERSEUS leaves Hamburg on May..."

A second, more careful reading did not change the contents. I looked up and met my father's glance.

"I go to Ecuador," I announced.

*   *   *   *   *

I had little more than a month to prepare. A friend drove my parents and me to Hamburg. On board the PERSEUS we met representatives of the firm I was to join in Ecuador and other passengers shipping out together with me. In the late afternoon my parents and I said good-bye, the ship separated from the pier and began the voyage downstream the river Elbe.

It tried to envision the new life opening up for me. As the coast of Germany disappeared in the evening glow, Germany also dwindled from my mind.

I settled in my stateroom. *The past is the past. The future is what counts.*

Last pictures with my parents in Lubeck, 1955

My parents moved to Frankfurt where my father found employment in the fur trade. He had been able to settle all debts and close out the business in Lübeck.

On board the PERSEUS, May 1955

Appendix

Excerpts from an eye witness report of the air attacks on Seestadt Rostock, April 24 through 28, 1942.

Condensed and translated from BOMBEN AUF ROSTOCK, Hans-Werner Bohl,

ISBN 3861670712, Konrad Reich, Kappen-Pott-Weg 7, Rostock-Brinkmansdorf.

Approach of two British waves had been reported. The first attack was expected any minute. We heard the Flak from Warnemünde and now our Rostocker opened up. Last night, mostly industrial targets were hit with explosive bombs; now a hailstorm of incendiary bombs fell on residential sectors. We (messengers) rushed to direct rescue to St. Georgstrasse and Alexandrinenstrasse where five- and six-story buildings stood in flames and we saw the beautiful Steintor burning like a huge torch.

A terrible explosion threw us to the pavement. Some houses at the corner of Paulstrasse were hit. Bricks, glass and branches flew through the air in the strong wind, and trees snapped. We got up and stumbled over piles of debris. I helped rescuers evacuating burning homes. We carried belongings to the Reiferbahn (a park along Paulstrasse) to keep the street free for emergency vehicles.

The air raid continued in all its fury. Trucks with helpers from outside the city arrived to give assistance where most urgently needed. I saw the Nicolai Kirche engulfed in flames.

Fifteen houses on Wismarsche Strasse were burning. The façade of one house collapsed. A chunk of concrete killed one of my comrades.

91

(The following night.)

The sirens sounded again. The English had no difficulty in finding the city. The fires, aided by the wind, showed them the way. We thought the previous nights were terrible, but it got much worse. Within fifteen minutes all hell broke loose. Our Flak fired on the enemy, with little effect. From a window in the attic I saw the planes approach low over the old city and sow incendiary bombs as far as to the Kröpeliner Tor. The entire inner city, from the Rosegarden to the Warnow, was burning.

It was hard for a Rostocker to see his town in flames—the streets, the beautiful houses, and the churches in ruins.

Both ends of General-Litzmannstrasse were burning and one house had collapsed into the street. I climbed across the rubble and removed burning beams from an intersection to let trucks pass to the Katholische Klinik. Beds and blankets and the patients were loaded into the trucks and they drove off.

The post office was on fire, but first we had to help at the Frauen Klinik in Friedrich-Franzstrasse. The women patients were transferred to the house on the other side of the street.

I rode my bike through the burning Grüner Weg to Paulstrasse to see if the rescue of the patients in the Catholic Clinic had been completed. A wall of heat came towards me. Paulstrasse was burning on both sides of the Tonhalle (a restaurant), which had received a direct hit. French POWs, located in a camp behind the Tonhalle, were trying to stop the fire from spreading. There were twenty-five to thirty casualties.

We expected reinforcements from Warnemünde and Doberan. Fire engines were waiting outside the city for the attack to stop. Fire trucks had come from as far as Berlin and Hamburg and from many other towns and villages.

I watched the old, beautiful gables—the pride of Rostock—as they crumbled and fell. Fire spread across the ancient city. The old homes were engulfed in flames. Fire engine companies tried hopelessly to stem the inferno with water sucked from the Warnow.

Refugees clogged the roads from the city. In the evening military field kitchens rolled into town and dispensed warm food.

Excerpts of the report by Captain Semjon M. Dmitrewski of the 65th (Soviet) Army, the first to enter Rostock at noon of May 1, 1945.
Condensed and translated from BOMBEN AUF ROSTOCK, Hans-Werner Bohl,
ISBN 3861670712, Konrad Reich, Kappen-Pott-Weg 7, Rostock-Brinkmansdorf.

In the early morning of May 1, the commander of my regiment gave me the order to take Rostock by storm to cut off the retreating flood of enemy troops along the coast. In Tessin (small town some 10 miles southeast of Rostock) I discussed with the commander of a tank battalion how best to combine our efforts to accomplish the task. I decided to put two companies of my battalion on the tanks, together with the 45 mm guns. The third company and the mortar company were distributed onto the vehicles. We took off at high speed over open terrain, avoiding the roads. Stopping to ascertain the situation, we gathered all our troops. Then we hurried on. "Dajosh Rostock!"

At Brinkmansdorf (suburb of Rostock) I sent one tank ahead to find out the condition of the Mühlendamm Brücke. Suddenly we lost contact. After waiting a few minutes, we went forward again. In Brinkmansdorf a man stopped us and called out that the bridge had been blown up and that we should use the Petri Brücke. I considered: is it a trap, or honest advice? I sent a group ahead to verify the information, but time was of the essence and I decided to trust the man who seemed credible to me. On our approach to the Petri Bridge, we receive some fire, but it was not serious and we crossed without a problem. The bridge was prepared with explosives, but did not blow up.

Without further resistance, the first two companies, the artillery and the mortars took positions along the Warnow in order to cut off retreat. The third company and the tanks continued to the western outskirts of the town and established positions to guard our rear. No real fight with the enemy took place, although we knew of the order to defend Rostock to the end, but the Nazis had fled and there was hardly any resistance. At dusk a few shots were fired from some houses, but we accomplished our task with few casualties. The escape route to the west was cut. The tanks continued westward while we remained in Rostock.

White rags were displayed from the houses that were still occupied. We had the clear impression that the pile of rubble once must have been a beautiful city.

My Home

1. Where the Baltic Sea Waves tumble towards the Strand,
    Where the yellow Seagrass grows in fine, white Sand,
    :,:Where the Seagulls scream o'er breaking Seas of Foam,
    That's where I belong, that's where I'm at Home. :,:

2. Wind and Waves have sung my Childhood Melodies,
    In the Dunes I laughed, I cried, I skinned my Knees;
    :,: But I longed to see the strange and distant Lands,
    Sail the open Oceans, fly and take my Chance. :,:

3. All that Life could give me through the Years I found.
    All my Heart's Desires I can hardly count.
    :,: All my youthful Yearnings I've put to the Test,
    Calmed all my Desires - yet, I'm not at Rest. :,:

4. Longing, yearning, dreaming of my Fatherland,
    Where the Waves keep rolling to the pure, white Sand,
    :,: Where the Seagulls scream o'er breaking Seas of Foam, -
    That's where I belong, that's where I'm at Home. :,:

translated from the original
low-German text MINE HEIMAT
by Martha Müller-Grälert
by: Peter Haase